BALTHUS
IN HIS OWN WORDS

601 West 26th Street, 18th floor
New York, NY 10001
USA
Tel.: 212 989-6810 Fax: 212 647-0005
www.assouline.com

First published by Editions Assouline, Paris, France.

Translated from the French by David Wharry.
Proofreading: Margaret Burnham

Color separation: Gravor (Switzerland)
Printed by Grafiche Milani (Italy)

ISBN: 2 84323 301 1

BALTHUS
IN HIS OWN WORDS

A CONVERSATION WITH
CRISTINA CARRILLO DE ALBORNOZ

ASSOULINE

a

Adam-Maxwell Reweski

The founder of my family, a Lebonski (they are very well-known in Poland), was a powerful lord. He left my brother and me a sum of money that we could use for our education if we became Catholics. And we did convert to Catholicism, whereas my father was a Protestant. Unfortunately, when my brother and I came of age to inherit the money, we were in Germany and it was no longer worth a cent *(he laughs)*.

Artist

I detest the word "artist" and find the word "creation"—so often used by those who call themselves artists—pretentious. In *Tintin,* I find it amusing that Captain Haddock's ultimate insult is always "Artist!" As Picasso once said: "I am not an artist." As for me, I would simply call myself a craftsman. The word artist is synonymous with individualism and the assertion of one's personality, two predominant notions in today's society. I remember a Polish painter once asked, "What must one do to paint?" I replied that the first thing to do was forget oneself and quickly get rid of one's personality. The important thing is anonymity. He who believes in personality remains unclear. Of course, people often say, "One must be oneself." But what is "oneself"? Who really knows?

"Poisonality," as the Americans say, is one of the plagues of modernism. What I find likeable about Americans is that they don't really have a past. Modernity, which began in the true sense with the Renaissance, determined the tragedy of art. The artist emerged as an individual and the traditional way of painting disappeared. From then on the artist sought to express his inner world, which is a limited universe: He tried to place his personality in power and used painting as a means of self-expression. But great painting has to have universal meaning. This is sadly no longer so today and this is why I want to give painting back its lost universality and anonymity, because the more anonymous painting is, the more real it is. The oriental philosopher Kumala Suami explains all this admirably. In particular, he recalls the Middle Ages, when there was no frontier between Western and Oriental art and when the artist was also much more in contact with the spiritual world, the world of God. But after the Renaissance, everything centered around man and personality. The universality of medieval painting stepped aside to make way for the primacy of the individual. This decline of Western art was slow and gradual, but it led finally to forgetting the love of painting for painting's sake.

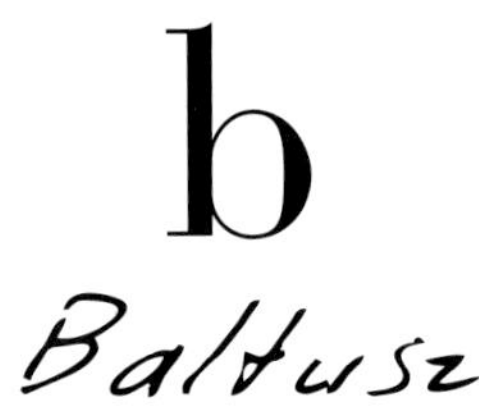

This was the Christian name of one of my Polish cousins, a Rzweski who had a habit of going around on a camel and was rather eccentric. When I was born, my parents were expecting a girl. They hadn't thought about a boy's name, so they called me Baltusz after my cousin. When I began signing my paintings with this name, I found out there was a Belgian painter with the same name. So I changed the spelling from Baltusz to Balthus.

Beauty

I'm for beauty at a time when beauty is unappreciated. Dostoyevsky said, "Beauty will save the world." For me, beauty and nature are linked. If God was content with the world he created, it was because it was beautiful. In my painting, I try to express divine beauty, which is very difficult today because people are only interested in ugliness. I think God has been forgotten. *Tutto è brutto...*

I find it unbearable to think that so many places that used to be so pleasant have become industrial sites or megalopoliscs with no architecture, full of noise and machines. The Paris I once knew no longer exists. In some ways, my painting depicts a world that has disappeared. Nothing could be further from me than the taste for horror. This is what separates me from expressionism or gifted painters such as Francis Bacon. I liked him a lot as a friend, but never managed to understand why he was fascinated by ugliness.

Bilboquet

While I was painting Pierre Leyris's portrait, his wife, who was present at the sittings, never stopped playing *bilboquet* (cup-and-ball game). The image has kept coming back to me in my dreams ever since.

Bonnard

It's said that he was my first mentor, yet his way of painting has nothing to do with mine. Bonnard and Derain were close friends of my family, but their conception of painting is very different from mine. They painted very quickly, whereas I constantly rework what I do. Antonin Artaud said I lingered too long in front of my canvases. I do believe one never really finishes a picture—the truth is it's fatigue which obliges one to stop. Bonnard often came to our house. One day, talking to my father about me, he said, "Whatever you do, never send him to an art school." That was his only influence. Bonnard was like a little boy. I remember one dinner in particular at his house. I must have been around twelve years old. Matisse, who was there, said to him, "Bonnard, you and I are the greatest painters of our time." Bonnard's face, usually so gay, fell, and with that doglike expression of his he replied, "It's awful what you're saying, Matisse. If we two are the greatest painters then we should be weeping with sadness."

My parents taught me nothing as far as painting goes, but they helped by giving me the culture necessary to become a painter. They personally knew all the painters of the time. The greatest artists of the beginning of the century all came to our house: Derain, Bonnard, Matisse, Nijinsky, Stravinsky… Even if my parents weren't able to help me materially, I am grateful to them for providing me with spiritual means and for helping me go in the right direction.

C

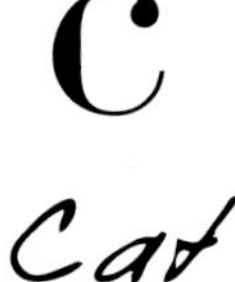

My first cat was called "Mitsou." Ever since, I have always lived surrounded by cats. Like them, I don't like obeying, and like them, I'm self-taught and don't like communal public places! Like me, they are sometimes cruel, but never vulgar. I assert my catlike nature: I used to be called "the king of cats."

Childhood

I had a very happy childhood and this obviously influenced my vision of painting and the world, which seemed more beautiful then than today. I read *Alice in Wonderland* and the stories in *Struwwelpeter*, which fascinated me. The romantic heroes, Baudelaire, Chateaubriand and Delacroix, were also part of my childhood. Today I still see things with the same enchantment. The adult vision of the world doesn't interest me. The only evolution my work has undergone has been a deepening of my conception of painting, which can be summed up in one word: universality. This evolution stems from my study of Piero della Francesca and his art of pictorial construction and also my discovery of Gustave Courbet.

My childhood was also marked by the richness of the intellectual and artistic circles my parents frequented. My father had a very fine collection of drawings by Delacroix and Daumier and Japancse paintings. Alas, we lost everything when we became Germans during the war.

Christianity

Christianity is the importance of Christ. My wife Setsuko wants to become Christian. I'm a Catholic myself and believe in resurrection. I'm a very religious person. My painting is a spiritual discipline; in some ways it's a prayer. I've always been surprised by how faithless and lawless society seems to be today, despite Malraux having said that the next century would be "a religious century or would not be at all."

Every Wednesday, my friend Mr. Burton, a very learned professor, and I organize a reading evening. Tonight we're going to read the Bible. We began with Plato, whose major work, in my opinion, is *The Banquet*. Love goes beyond the perceptible and love is a synonym for beauty in this book. Plato is a very great artist in the true sense of the word, that is he reconstructs the world and stamps meaning, or a direction, on it. Today we no longer have a direction or parameters. We find ourselves vulnerable. We are in a situation identical to the one the samurai call *happo yabure,* meaning "the enemy is attacking on all sides" or "we're surrounded."

Culo (ass)

Once, in Venice, I stopped someone in the street to ask him for a light: "*Mi dà un fuoco?*" He replied, "*Ti do anche il culo* (I can also give you my ass)." "*Fammi vedere* (Let me see it)," I said. "*Non mi piace!* (I don't like it)," he replied. Then I turned him round and touched his chest: "What about your *poppe* (nipples) then!"

d

Derain

I often went to his house in Paris. His studio, which he lent me so I could paint *The Mountain,* was just below mine in Cour de Rohan. It was packed with objects he collected from the Far East. Derain was enormous. I've always likened him to a cloud, with changing forms: He changed his opinions like shirts! He really was a charming man, and funny.

Doctorate

A few months ago, I was awarded an honorary doctorate in Poland. When I received the invitation, I asked myself, "Why me? What have I done to deserve this?" The day before I received the title, I was still hesitant about accepting it. But on the day, a wonderful cardinal, Monsignor Henryck Gulbinowicz, a friend of our Pope, said, "Forget who you are, think of your parents and Poland and accept this distinction in their honor." My father was a doctor. He wrote a very scholarly work on Daumier. I'm self-taught myself—which is why this doctorate seemed to me to be a misunderstanding. But I have to admit that I was very touched by it.

Dominican

My brother, Pierre, became a Dominican monk when he was young. Then, a lot later, he converted to Islam.

e

Embarrassment

I feel terribly embarrassed when I realize that after so many years spent painting I still don't know what painting is. I wanted to be a painter from a very early age, and my way of painting hasn't changed since then either. I still see things the way I saw them when I was twelve. I've never ceased marveling at what surrounds me.

Essere (to be)

Shakespeare: "To be or not to be."

f

Feudalism

Feudalism is the system I prefer, the one which lasted the longest in history. It was first and foremost a system based on the lord's duty to protect his subjects. If the lord failed in this duty, or if he proved himself unjust or cruel, he was immediately done away with. Human relationships based on protection please me a lot. The feudal era was also a time when the word aristocracy had real meaning, a genuine *raison d'être* since it guaranteed the respect of Christian values like fidelity and faith.

I believe I'm a profoundly medieval man. In fact, I was made a *Grande Croce* (Grand Cross) of the Order of Saints Maurice and Lazarus, a knighthood of the arts and letters of House of Savoy. Setsuko was made a Dame Grand Cross *("I'd want to accompany you even to hell," the countess adds. Balthus laughs and recites Dante: "Amor, ch'a nullo amato amar perdona.")*

A romantic vision of the Middle Ages? No, I'd say instead that I don't share the idea that the Middle Ages were dark and decadent. I created worlds that became real for me simply because I believed in them. This sometimes causes confusion between vision and reality, but all my visions constitute my existence. In the end, what is reality? I myself believe that reality reinvents itself with each moment.

France

My family has been very attached to France for generations. For me, a painter, France serves as a reference: great painting has nearly always been French.

I particularly admire Courbet, who is, to my mind, one of the greatest French painters.

His incredible genius resides in his ability to identify with and represent objects. This enables him to go beyond the stage of vulgar realism.

When he paints snow, for example, we can smell it, we perceive its very substance. I admire his way of painting young girls, their thoughts and outer expressions as human beings opening to the world, while already having a true inner and sentimental life of their own.

g

Giacometti

Alberto Giacometti was like a brother to me, and I miss him a lot. He was a very gentle person with whom I above all had a real working dialogue.
His disappearance was dramatic for me because I've had nobody to talk to since.
It was André Breton who first brought him to my home in Paris. We became friends immediately and remained so, linked by the same disdain for the Surrealists and a certain, inflexible vision. We both went against trends. Alberto sought the same thing as me; we were interested in the past, in tradition and wanted to work from nature, rather like Cézanne did. When Giacometti began working from nature, he abandoned Surrealism. Breton reproached him for it, saying, "But everyone knows it's a head." To which Alberto replied, "Not me, and placing the eye in its exact place is precisely what interests me."

Goya

I have the utmost admiration for his painting. It is so vast it can't be reduced and it is, above all, as fantastic as his own life. It has everything: his love for the Duchess of Alba, the customs of his time, the brutality of war, even his mocking attitude towards the queen. His portrait of the royal family is splendid, like a bunch of flowers.

Great Britain

I love Great Britain. I feel close to this country for two reasons. My first language was English and I have Scottish ancestors. My

grandmother was a Gordon, from the same lineage as Lord Byron. I love the elegant British lifestyle, and what is known as the British stiff upper lip. The capacity to keep a cool head under all circumstances is totally foreign to me, which explains why it fascinates me. I am a very emotional man, perhaps too much so… My youth was an absolute whirlwind of feelings, exactly like Emily Bronte's *Wuthering Heights,* which I illustrated. I was completely at home in this novel. It described my youth perfectly. I was in love with Antoinette—de Watteville—and I was determined to win her. But Antoinette, on top of being a difficult girl, was already engaged to someone else. I reread her letters every evening. I think that, like Heathcliff, I didn't want to leave adolescence.
I still have this romanticism in me. I am a marvelous person—in the 18th-century sense—*(he laughs)* that is, a possessive and robust person like my relative Lord Byron. *("He has always lived in a great atmosphere of love and passion. He's the absolute flame," Setsuko adds.)* I am always in love with what I do. One can't have too much love.

h

Harumi

That's the name I gave my daughter. It means "spring beauty." She finds it a bit hard to live up to, but she deserves it!

Homer

I've just read a translation of *The Iliad* in Swiss German. It was very interesting, particularly because the author perfectly captured and interpreted the ancient dialects and different terms used in Ancient Greece.

Hugo

Oh! Combien de marins, combien de capitaines
Qui sont partis joyeux pour de courses lointaines
Dans ce morne horizon se sont évanouis!
Combien ont disparu, dure et triste fortune!
Dans une mer sans fond, par une nuit sans lune
Sous l'aveugle Océan à jamais enfouis!

O how many sailors, how many captains
Cheerfully departed for distant climes
Into that gloomy horizon did vanish!
How many disappeared, cruel and sad fortune!
Into a bottomless sea on a moonless night
Beneath the blind Ocean forever buried!

(*Océano Nox*, 1836.)

Here, in the Grand Chalet, we have a Victor Hugo room. He stayed in this 18th-century house from time to time, which used to be a hotel. After living in Italy, Setsuko and I moved to Switzerland and had tea here one day, in what today is our home. The countess adored the place because it reminded her of Japanese houses made of wood. Pierre Matisse, my gallery owner, arranged everything to enable us to buy it. In return, I agreed to paint five pictures, *View of Montecalvello*, *The Painter and His Model*, *Sleeping Nude* and two *Standing Nude*.

i

Ideograms

The Chinese characters. I know a few. Ideograms help a lot with drawing and knowing how to paint. The character is executed in a limited space, which leads one to call on one's sense of precision and aesthetics. The word "rest," for instance, is composed of the words "man" and "tree." Wonderful! I think it would be very useful to teach the art of ideograms in Western art schools because it sharpens the sense of equilibrium in composition. I've never been to China, but I lived in the heart of the Swiss Alps when I was small, in the Wattenburg mountains. While reading a Chinese book one day, I discovered that the Chinese see things appearing and disappearing in the mountains just like me. I am drawn to Asian art because of its universal aspect, which Western art doesn't have. Unfortunately, few painters are interested in Chinese painting these days. I am also fascinated by its economy. As for ancient Japanese painting, it's strange how much it resembles the Siena School. My interest in the East intensified a great deal when I met the countess *(Setsuko, his Japanese wife)*. If, during this century, Western man, instead of turning to African art, had looked at Oriental art, the history of art would have been completely different!

I've understood

I've understood that stupidity is increasing in our world like an avalanche. I'm a pessimist. *"Grande mostruosa" (he goes on singing* Don Giovanni).

j

Japan

I love Japan. It's a very complex country. The language is incredibly funny; the comic and the sacred are very closely linked. We met the emperor. I was very moved because he remembered our visit when he was still crown prince, during which he showed Harumi two goldfish. Japan is also a country where, as Roland

Barthes, the author of *The Empire of Signs*, wrote, "ritual has real status." Daily ritual above all is very profound. It embodies the sacred. In Japan, there is also a respect for institutions. When a prince is not very intelligent, one says, "But he's the emperor!" It's both terrible and moving.

Journal (Delacroix)

Anyone interested in painting should read Delacroix's *Journal*. He writes about everything, from mixing colors to the advantage of painting from memory to capture the essence of objects. He also explains that he wasn't a romantic but a classicist. Picasso, who like me dreamed of the idea of the universal artist, did a lot of copies from Delacroix. "Delacroix, what a painter!" he would say, "and Picasso does nothing..."

k

Kimono

I was given my first kimono in the fifties, when I first visited Japan to prepare an exhibition devoted to this garment. It has been part of my daily wardrobe ever since. It is a very comfortable garment and suits me. I think it's a pity the kimono isn't worn more because it represents a very beautiful tradition. And I am a man of tradition. Setsuko, although she had a traditional Japanese education, is influenced by modern, Western fashion. I told her she has to go on wearing the kimono, which she has done.

Kuas

"Kuas" and not "Klo," is the proper pronunciation of my surname, Klossowski, which means "corn cob." It's a very old Slavic name that also exists in Russian. My father was furious when people said "Klo." He was proud of being Polish. I loved him very much.

Kurosawa

I admired him a great deal. He was profoundly feudalist, attached to the true traditions, to the true Japanese spirit and the spiritual side of existence. In *Ran*, he shows one event and three realities. In *Dersu Uzala*, he shows pure beauty.

L

Lion

When I was director of the Villa Medici, I was good friends with the director of the Rome zoo. He invited me to visit him there and asked for a lion cub to be brought out of its cage for me. The young lion never stopped licking me. Everyone kept shouting in terror. I said, "Be quiet! You'll scare the animal!"

Louis XIV

The Sun King was a true king, even if one has to admit that absolute power is a great danger for everyone. He was a very polite person. There is a wonderful anecdote about a Spanish ambassador who came to greet him and didn't take his hat off. The king pointed this impoliteness out to him. Yet, as an ambassador, he was perfectly within his rights. "I know, I know, Monsieur de Watteville," he said, "but there are ladies here."

Louis XIV was a highly trained and cultivated person, who contributed enormously to the prestige of French art throughout the world. He had a remarkable collection of works by Nicolas Poussin. Under Louis XIII, Poussin had lived in France, but he soon left the

kingdom because he was made to paint things unworthy of him, particularly minor commissions.
In my view, the French Revolution marked the beginning of the end. It consecrated the rise of the bourgeoisie, the idea of profit and the encouragement of personal enrichment. It was, in fact, the birth of today's world.

m

Malraux

He is one of the most important people in my life. He often invited me to his house, where we talked for hours on end. Malraux was my intellectual guide. He appointed me director of the Villa Medici, which was one of the happiest periods of my life. He was also indirectly responsible for my meeting Setsuko.

Mirror

The mirror is extremely important in my work. It allows me to see everything the other way around and to detect every fault.
It's been said that I made my models hold a mirror, or that I placed a mirror in my pictures to suggest dreaming, but this wasn't my intention at all. Dreams don't interest me.

Mozart

Mozart was an absolute genius. He had an infinite capacity to create the sublime. *(He starts singing* Don Giovanni *again, and other opera arias he knows by heart.)*
I want my painting, just like Mozart's music, to have a structure that the public finds familiar, but to produce a supernatural result at the same time. His works have everything, a passionate

character which seems to place them above real-life situations, while at the same time being close to real life and true feelings. This paradox produces a shock so intense it renders Mozart's *œuvre* unique. He is the Shakespeare of music.

n

Napoleon Bonaparte

Chateaubriand wrote, "Now that Napoleon, the most extraordinary figure of our time, is dead, what remains? We have nothing left." When one reads Chateaubriand, Napoleon seems fascinating, but it's still difficult to picture who he really was, outside of his genius for war. In his extraordinary book *Mémoires d'outre-tombe*, Chateaubriand describes meeting Napoleon. On his return from Egypt, struck by a religious transformation, he summoned Chateaubriand and they discussed religion's extraordinary power and formidable capacity to create meaning, to give life meaning. Chateaubriand was moved by the emperor's simplicity and also struck by his beauty. At the end of his reign, Napoleon was a fat man whose weakness was very well portrayed in *War and Peace* (Tolstoy): Prince Andrei realizes the emperor has disguised himself so that he can escape the Russian army incognito. Napoleon was no longer the Bonaparte of his glory days. Only the legend remained.

o

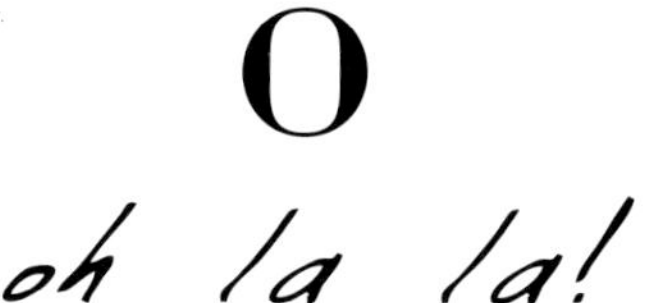

After a performance of *Attila*, by Pierre Corneille, there was so much confusion that the only criticism was "Oh la la!"

Otto of Austria

Baladine, my mother, knew him very well.
They met in a hat shop, where she was choosing some hats for her children.
She looked at him and exclaimed, "But it's Otto, of course!"
They became friends immediately.
My mother was very beautiful, and she had great charm.

p

Pertinent

It's the opposite of impertinent. I used to be very impertinent.
It shows clearly in the photos Irving Penn took of me. I wielded impertinence as much out of pleasure as to protect myself from people who didn't like me.
In Paris—where I lived from 1940 to 1953—I was very isolated because I went against trends, but I never felt this solitude in a negative way.
True, just about everyone hated me, but this left me indifferent. This indifference in fact saved me and my painting from the dangerous mistakes of fashion.
For me, only painting mattered.
I couldn't care less about the rest.
Picasso was the first person to buy one of my paintings; it was *The Children.*
We often talked about painting together.
He liked my work a lot. I remember one evening in particular, when after having dinner with Paul Eluard and Matisse, we stayed on together with Laurence Bataille. Picasso heaped so many compliments on me, I blushed.

q

Quoi

This word was in vogue in Cocteau's entourage. He used it to punctuate every phrase. Although a brilliant talker, Cocteau never managed to rid himself of this linguistic mannerism. It was quite simply his way of talking. As for his painting, it was very bad.
Once, with Marie-Lo de Noailles, we were witnesses at the marriage of a young man who wanted to impress his parents-in-law by provoking them.
The young priest officiating was scandalized by the way the ceremony went. At the end of the service everybody was invited to sign the register. When it was Cocteau's turn, he said to the priest, "Jean Cocteau." The priest asked him to spell out his name. Cocteau was very embarrassed. I found it amusing because everyone was supposed to know him. He was the most famous artist at that time, the prince of the poets. The final twist of fate: Edith Piaf eclipsed Cocteau's death by dying the same day as him.

r

Rome

"Rome, the unique object of my resentment!" (Pierre Corneille)
I think a lot about Rome these days, about the time I was director of the Villa Medici. I have a certain nostalgia for the city, because it meant much more to me than seeing beauty—Rome wasn't new to me; I had lived there several times during my youth.
Rome marked my life in a magical way. It was very interesting, very stimulating and not just from a strictly pictorial point of view. I was

able to do so many things there. I restored the Villa Medici, which regained all its splendor. I organized exhibitions of my beloved Giacometti and Courbet. In short, it was the most intense period of my life. Setsuko often came to Rome, where we have many friends. Federico...Federico...Fellini (*he is on the brink of tears*).... To talk about him is too painful. He was an extraordinary person, an extravagant personality, unique. I adored what he said about me: "You are the guardian of a heritage where time has deposited the culture of art." We both shared the same desire to show a familiar and intimate world.

S

Self-taught

I am self-taught; I learned to paint by copying paintings in the Louvre, especially Poussin, who was in some respects my mentor. I love everything about him: his color, his angelic and timeless way of painting and of course his women, who greatly influenced my work. On my father's advice, I then left for Italy. I stayed with friends in Florence. I was very young at the time, but my father never stopped repeating that Piero della Francesca was the Cézanne of his time. The Quattrocento painters—Masolino da Panicale, Masaccio—taught me everything about composition and the geometry of a work. As for the rest, Piero della Francesca was too clever for me.

Setsuko

I met her during a trip to Japan, when I was the director of the Villa Medici. Against the wishes of the Quai d'Orsay (the French Foreign Ministry), André Malraux sent me there to prepare an exhibition of

Japanese art in Paris. In a way, I owe having known her to him. I am eternally grateful to him. Setsuko was twenty. I was struck by the great beauty of this *modern jaru* (modern girl). Since that day, she has become the pillar of my existence.

Smoking

I'm a heavy smoker. I've smoked ever since I've painted. I discovered one day, in a science magazine, that smoking had a beneficial effect on concentration. And it's true that it helps me concentrate on my work. I don't understand how the Renaissance painters managed to paint without smoking…

S.O.S.

I'm sending out an S.O.S. to save painting because the love of painting is dead. I even believe that painting doesn't exist anymore. I just can't understand what painters today are doing. It's called "contemporary art"…. For me, it's merely something executed without mastery. In painting, there are certainly no rules but there is nevertheless a technical mastery to be acquired. In the past, everyone possessed this mastery, right down to the least-gifted painter. Painting was a craft then. Today, to paint means to do absolutely anything at all. I remember when Mirò showed his latest paintings to Picasso, he said to him indignantly, "Mirò …at your age?"

Today people are ashamed to see popular traditions disappearing little by little. Great painting used to feed on popular art. There was no difference between the two. And when someone wanted to become a painter, he had to do an apprenticeship. I've known all the great masters of this century and they all bemoaned the same thing: The painter's craft has disappeared.

In the end, perhaps modernity consists in not knowing how to make phrases with paint.

The only modernity I admit to is in the sense that Baudelaire understood it.

...Certainly not for *Surrealists*, at any rate...

Switzerland

I've lived here so long I almost believe I'm Swiss.
I discovered this country during World War I. I could tell you so many things about it. Switzerland played an important role in my youth and I've kept returning here, almost by chance. What I like most here is the uncomplicated, peasant spirit which reigns in all strata of society. This is one of the only countries where culture and popular art are still truly alive.

t

Tàpies

I met him in Rome. He is the only painter today who arouses my interest, even if his conception is very far from mine and even if, in a general way, these new forms of representation don't attract me. Braque often talked about pictorial effect.
Well, it was in Tàpies' paintings that I discovered pictorial effect, or sometimes glimpsed it. Things are treated in depth in his work. His painting exudes such power, such density one believes one sees it move.
I particularly liked his black period. As for the story of the sock on his picture, I admit I don't appreciate it *(one of Tàpies' works is made out of a large sock)*.

U

Ulysses

Joachim du Bellay, a 16th-century poet, wrote, “Happy is he who, like Ulysses, went on a beautiful journey...” His journey is the one I prefer.

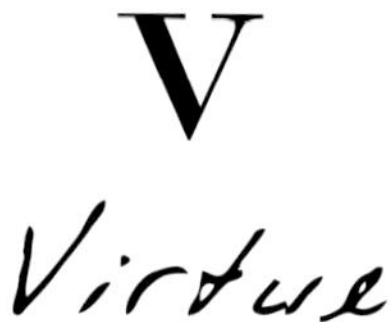

Virtue

Fidelity. The virtue I most appreciate is fidelity.

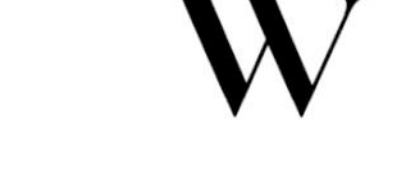

Watteville

Antoinette de Watteville was my first wife. I met her when I was four years old. Later, I wrote her beautiful letters. Her magnetism was extraordinary. She was an charming *femme fatale*. I loved everything about her: her beauty, her large eyes, her serenity, her confidence in herself, her aristocratic allure... The de Wattevilles were one of the most prestigious families in the Canton of Bern. Antoinette appears in *The Mountain* and *The White Skirt*. We were married in 1937 and have always remained friends.

Women

I could never paint a nude woman. I find the beauty of young girls more interesting and perfect than women’s. They embody becoming, a pre-being, in short they symbolize the most perfect beauty.

Woman is a being already situated in the world, whereas the adolescent—from the word *adolescere,* "to grow"—hasn't yet found her place. A woman's body is generally too defined; a girl's body is more beautiful *(he laughs)*. It's precisely this whole matter of young girls that has caused the misunderstanding about my painting. To classify my work as erotic is idiotic. Young girls are sacred, divine, angelic beings. Finally, the only thing poor Nabokov and I have in common is a sense of humor.

Y

Ying and Yang

Everything is based on ying and yang.

You

You, because I'm talking to you.

Z

Zen

"*Zen-zen. Wakarimasen deshita!*" ("I haven't understood a thing!") At the end of a lecture on this subject, it was with those words that a grand master of Japanese Zen answered when asked why he had remained silent.

Zouave

I discovered this word reading *Tintin,* which I adore. When Captain Haddock says to Professor Calculus that he's being a Zouave, he replies, "A Zouave! Me, a Zouave?"

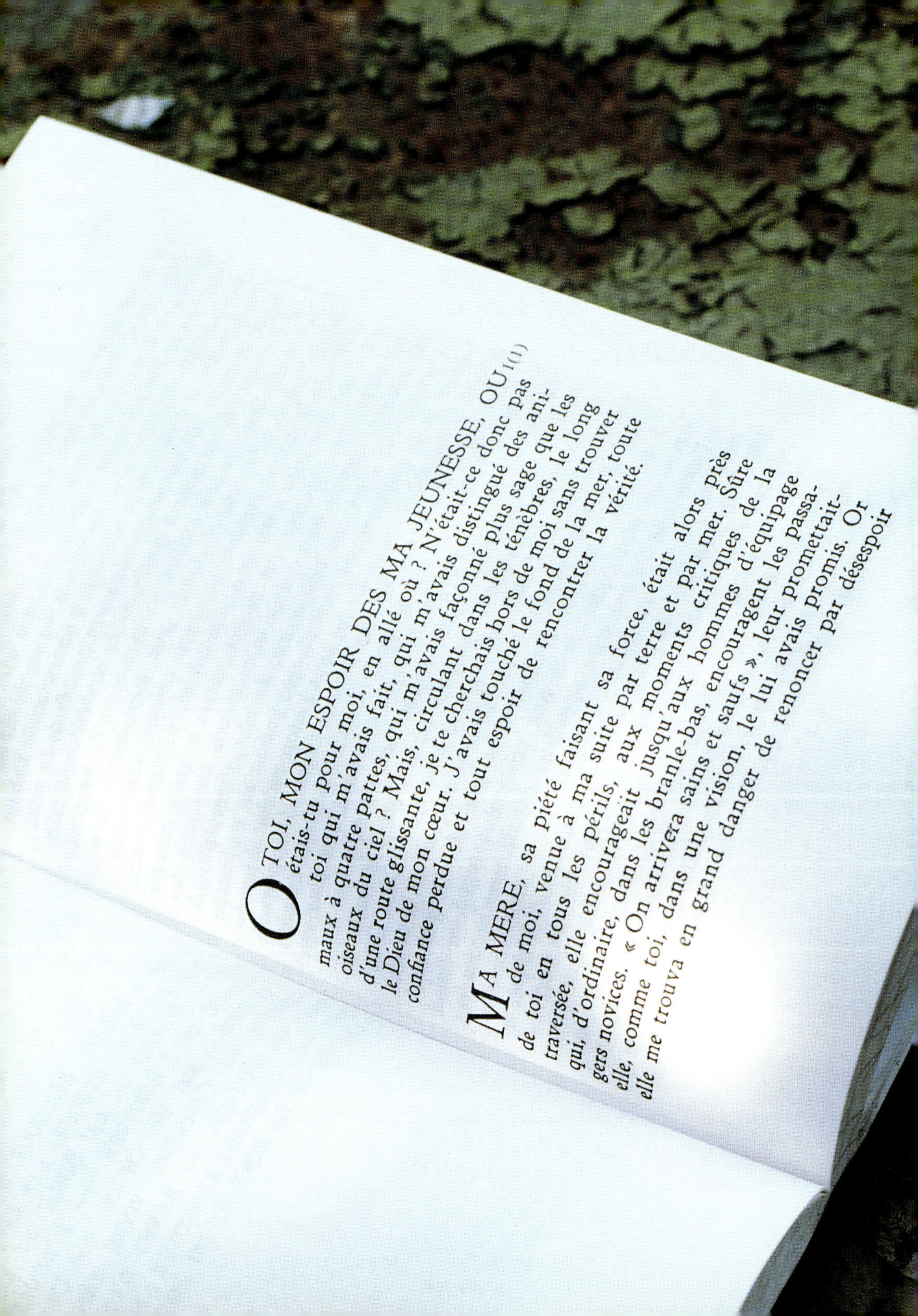

O TOI, MON ESPOIR DES MA JEUNESSE, OU[1](1) étais-tu pour moi, en allé où ? N'était-ce donc pas toi qui m'avais fait, qui m'avais distingué des animaux à quatre pattes, qui m'avais façonné plus sage que les oiseaux du ciel ? Mais, circulant dans les ténèbres, le long d'une route glissante, je te cherchais hors de moi sans trouver le Dieu de mon cœur. J'avais touché le fond de la mer, toute confiance perdue et tout espoir de rencontrer la vérité.

MA MERE, sa piété faisant sa force, était alors près de moi, venue à ma suite par terre et par mer. Sûre de toi en tous les périls, aux moments critiques de la traversée, elle encourageait jusqu'aux hommes d'équipage qui, d'ordinaire, dans les branle-bas, encouragent les passagers novices. « On arrivera sains et saufs », leur promettait-elle, comme toi, dans une vision, je lui avais promis. Or elle me trouva en grand danger de renoncer par désespoir

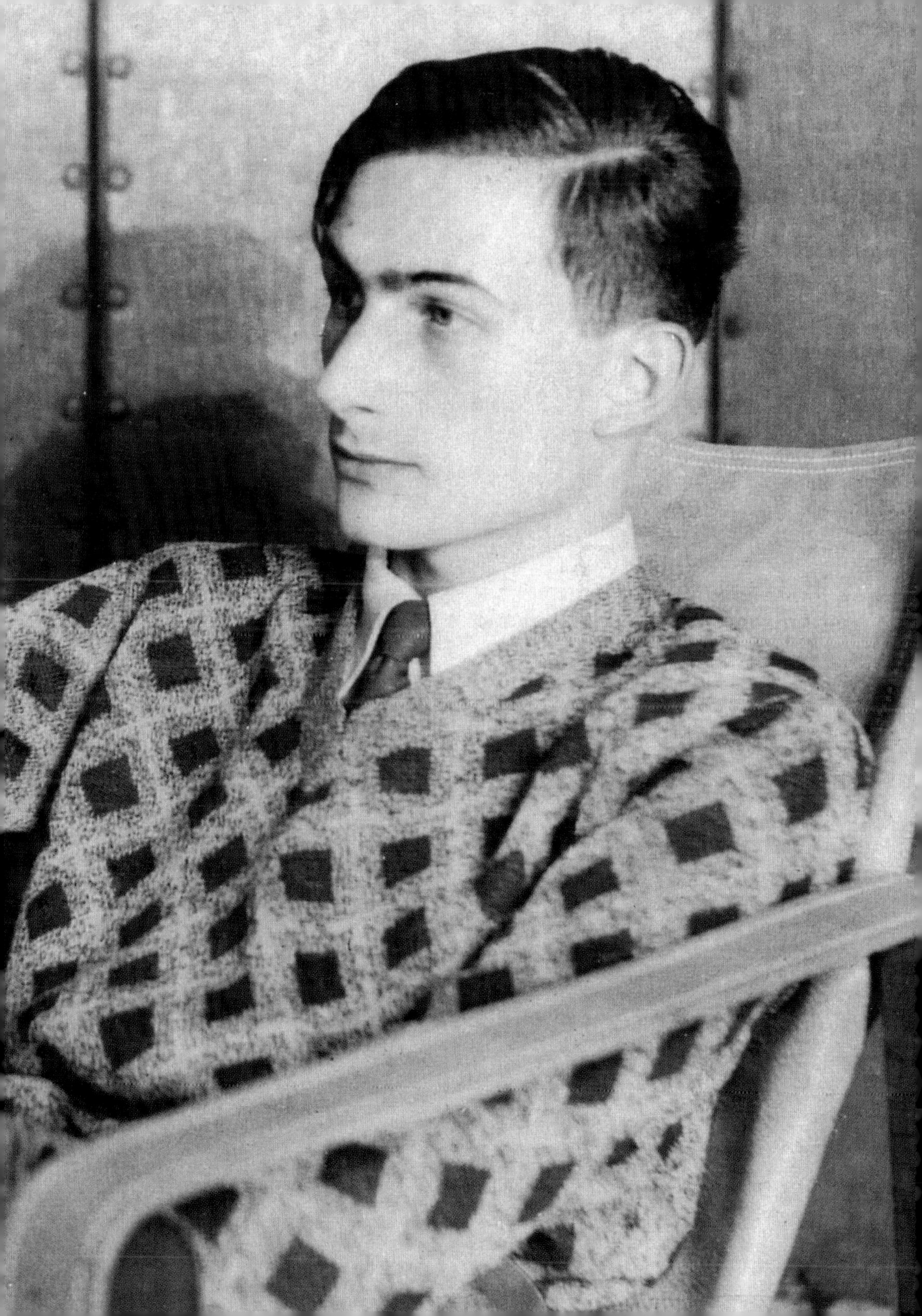

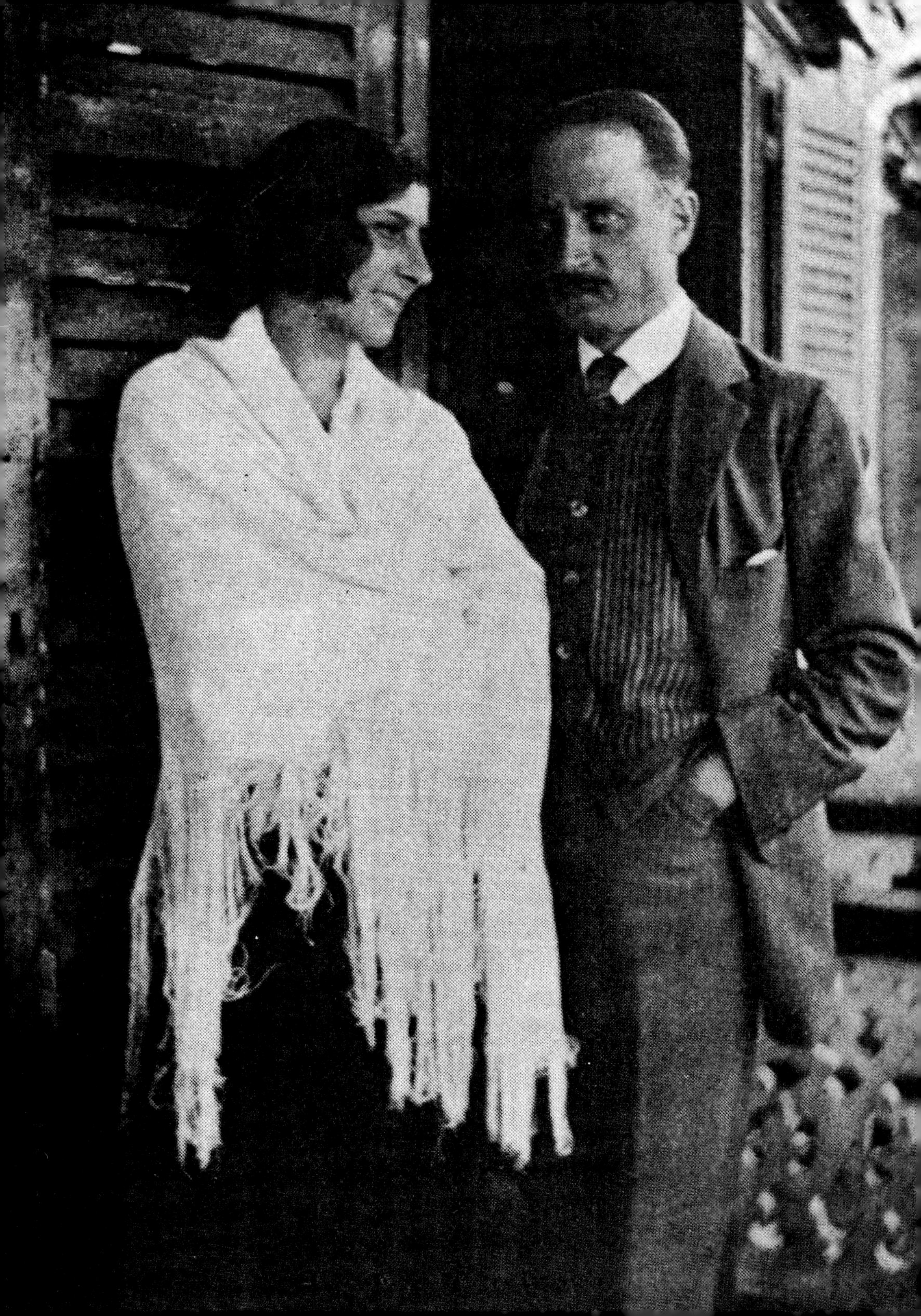

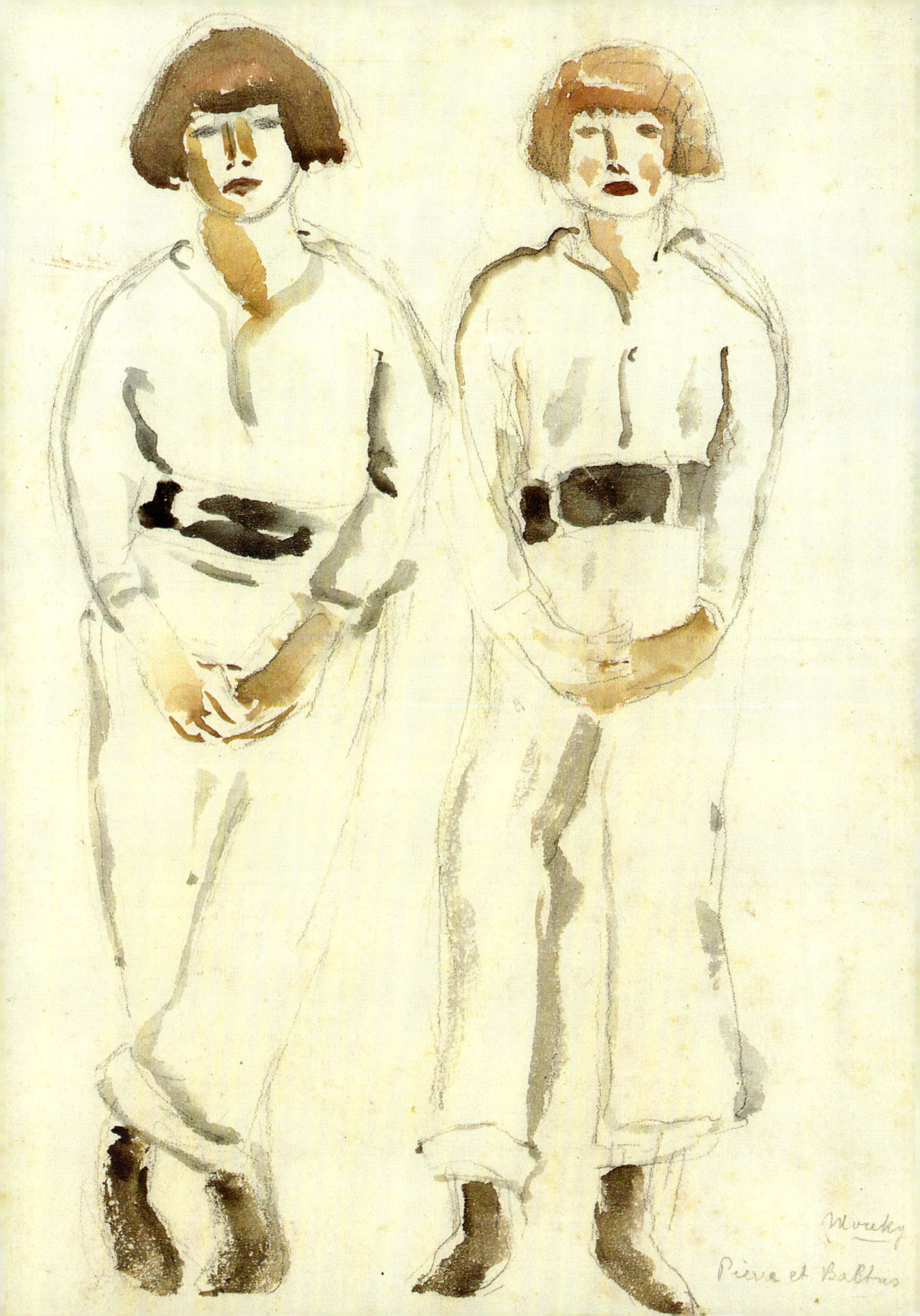
Mouky
Pierre et Baltus

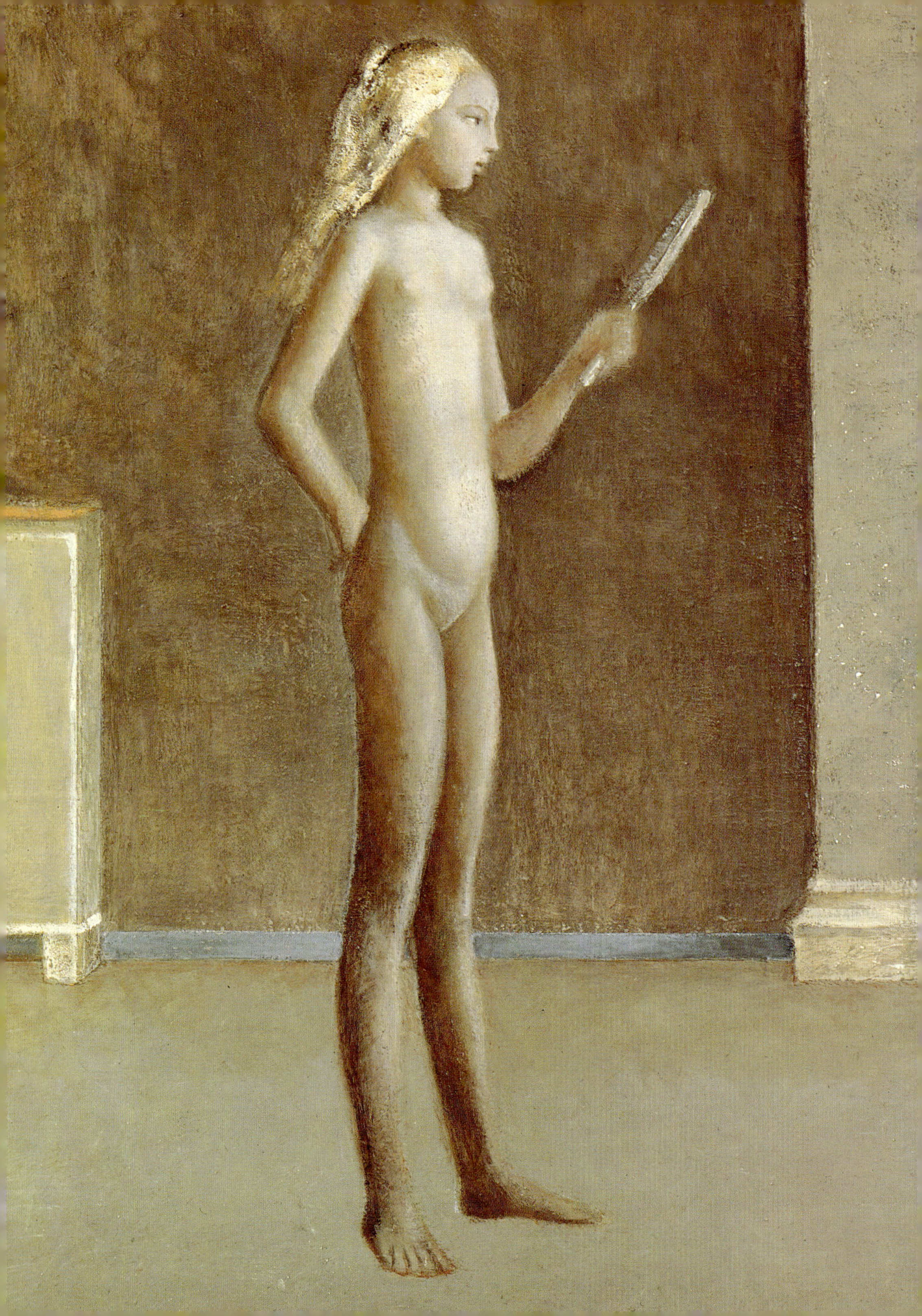

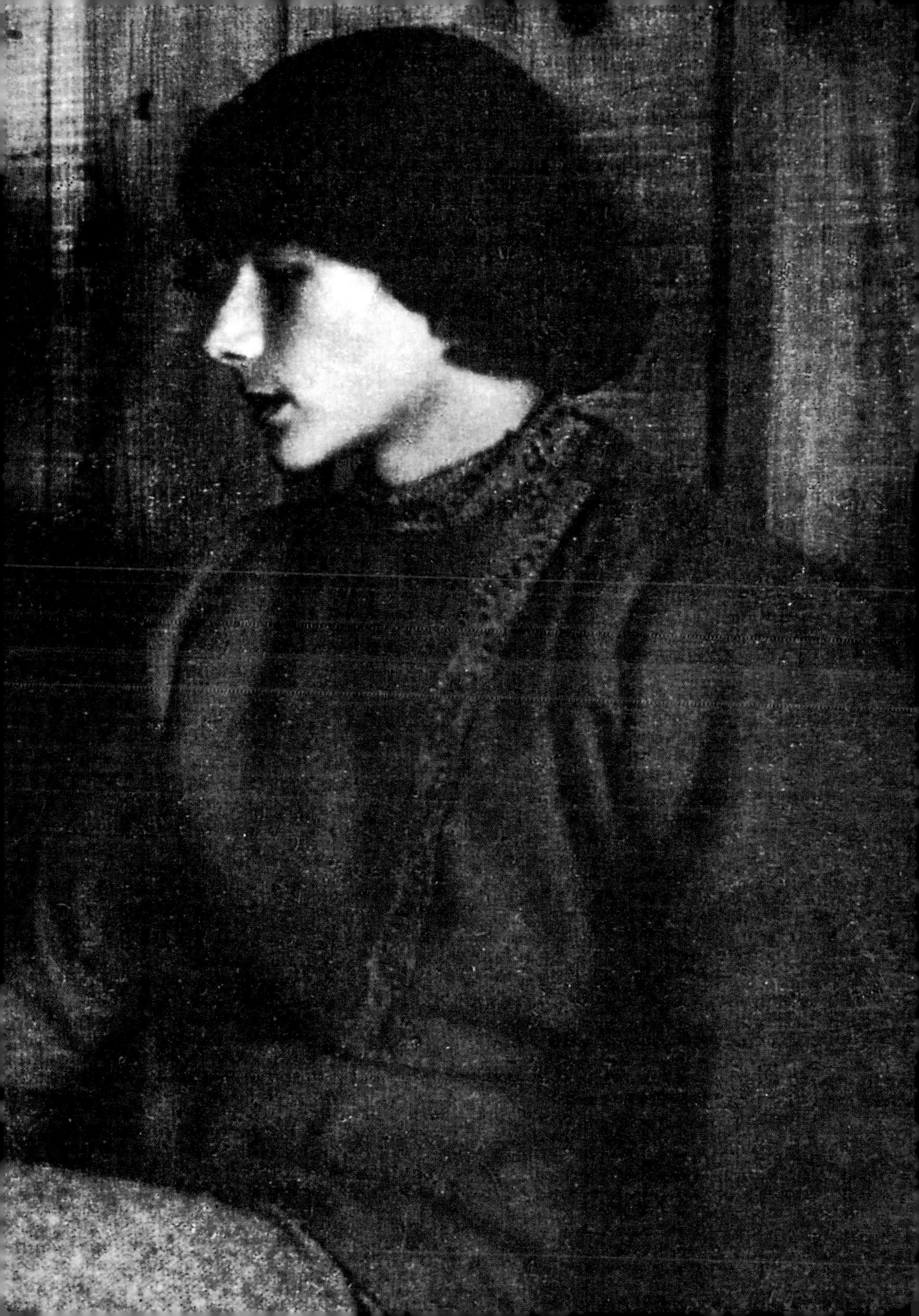

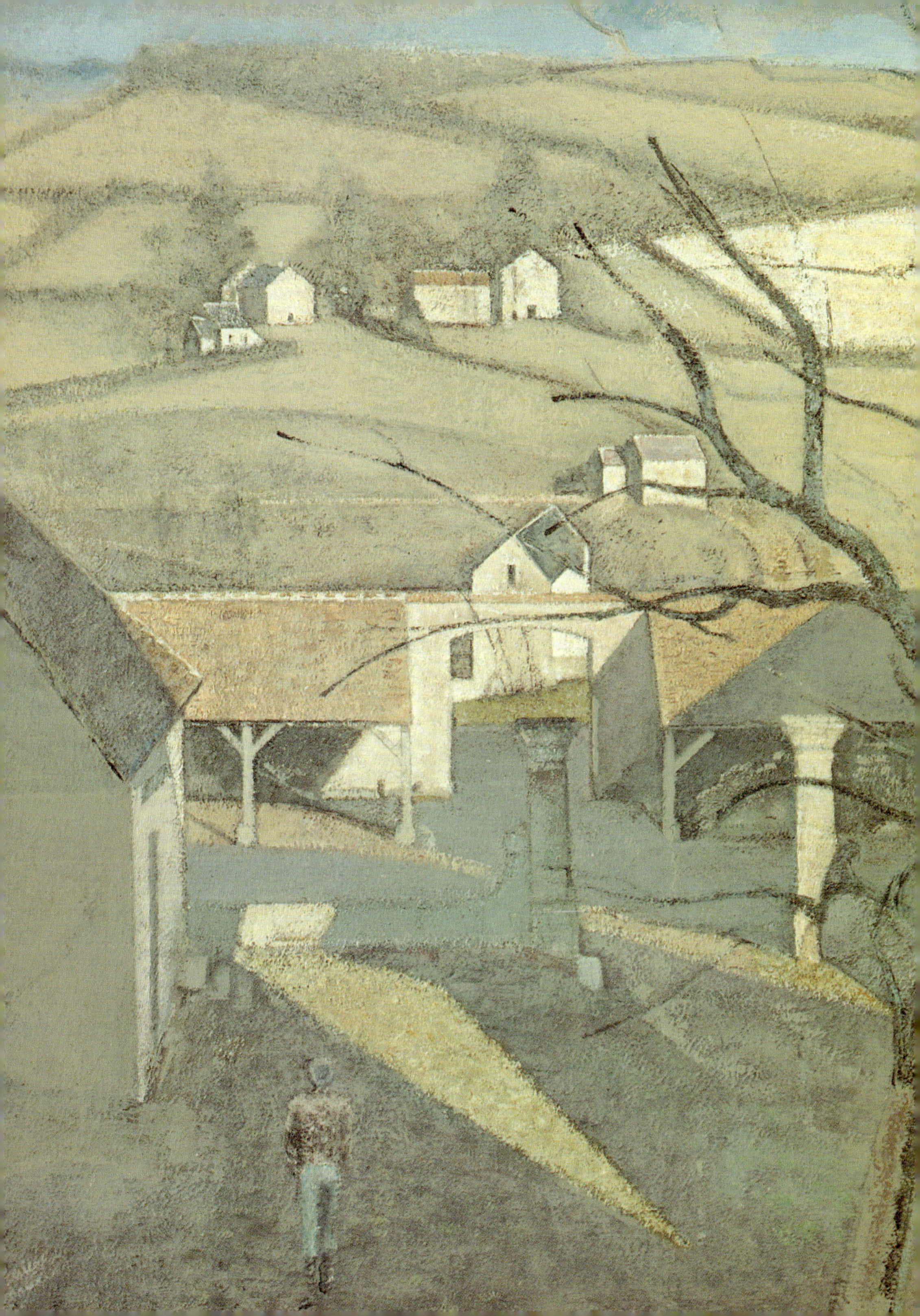

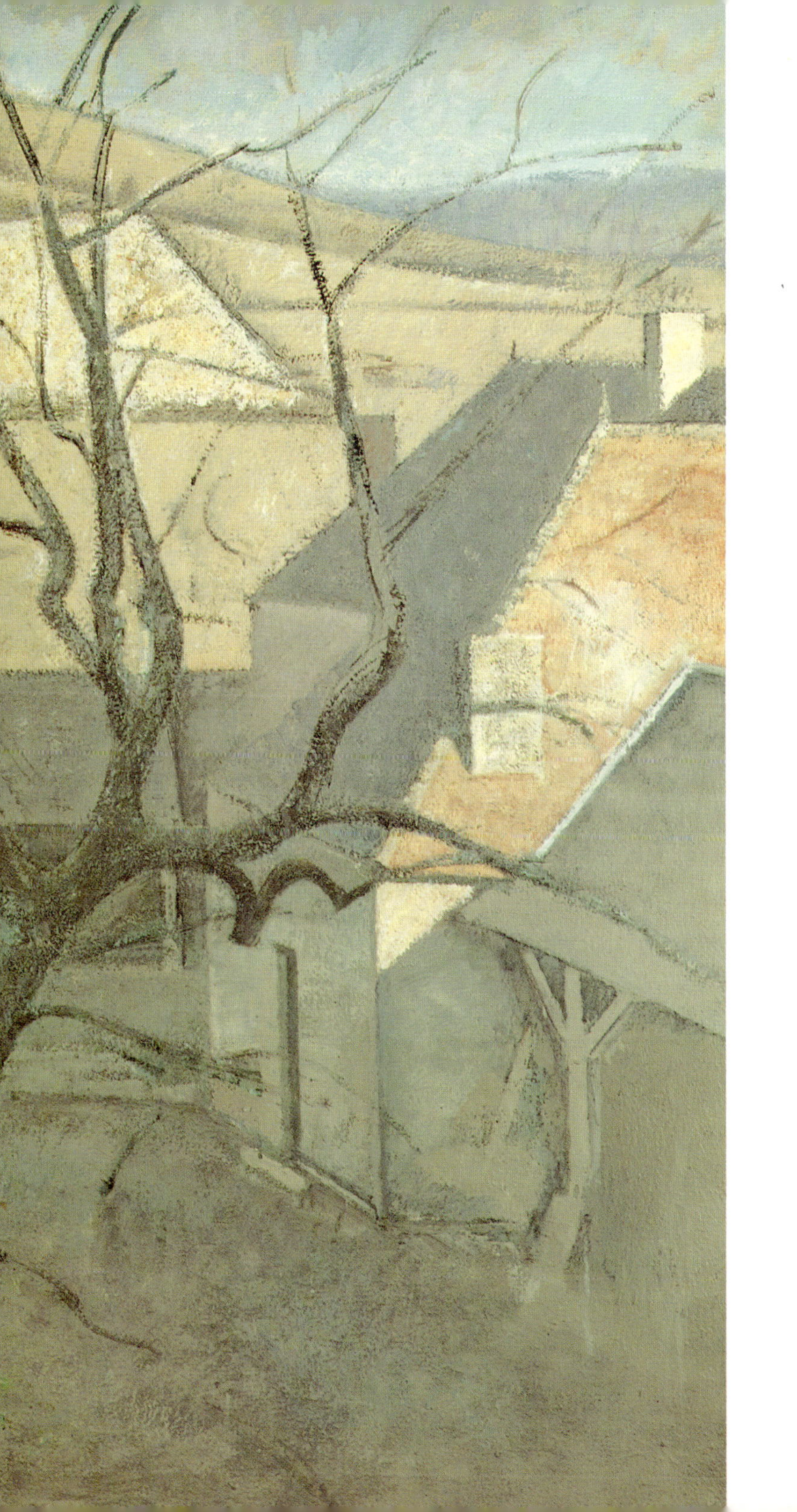

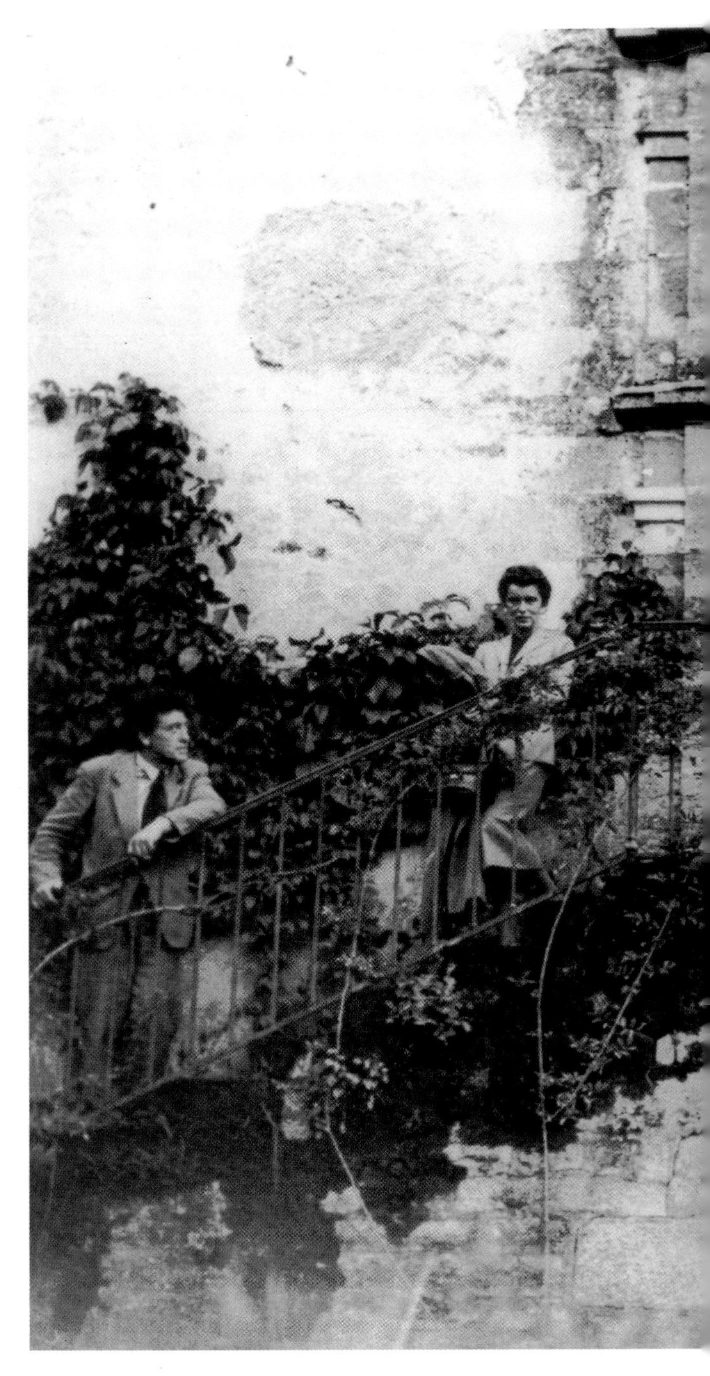

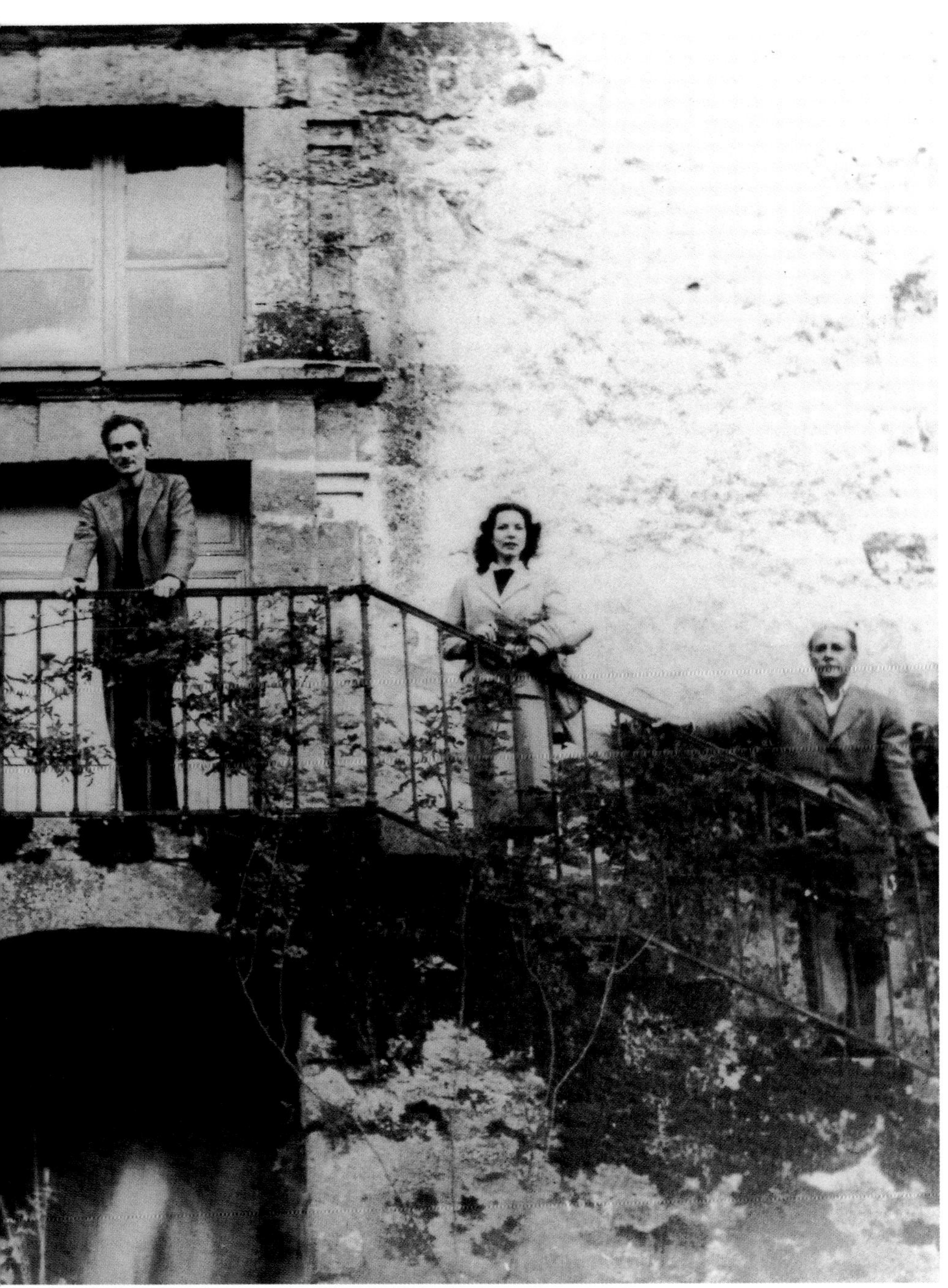

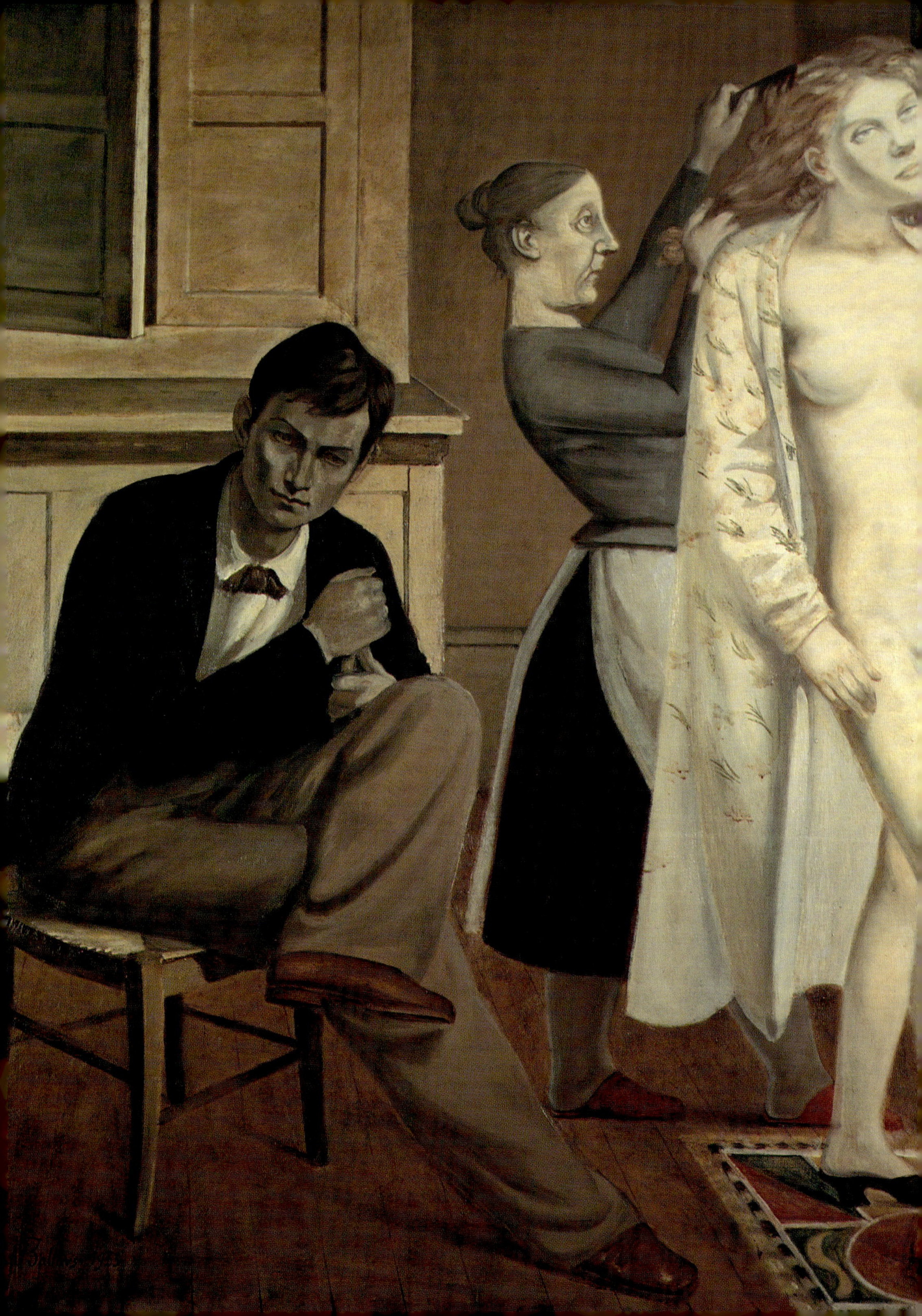

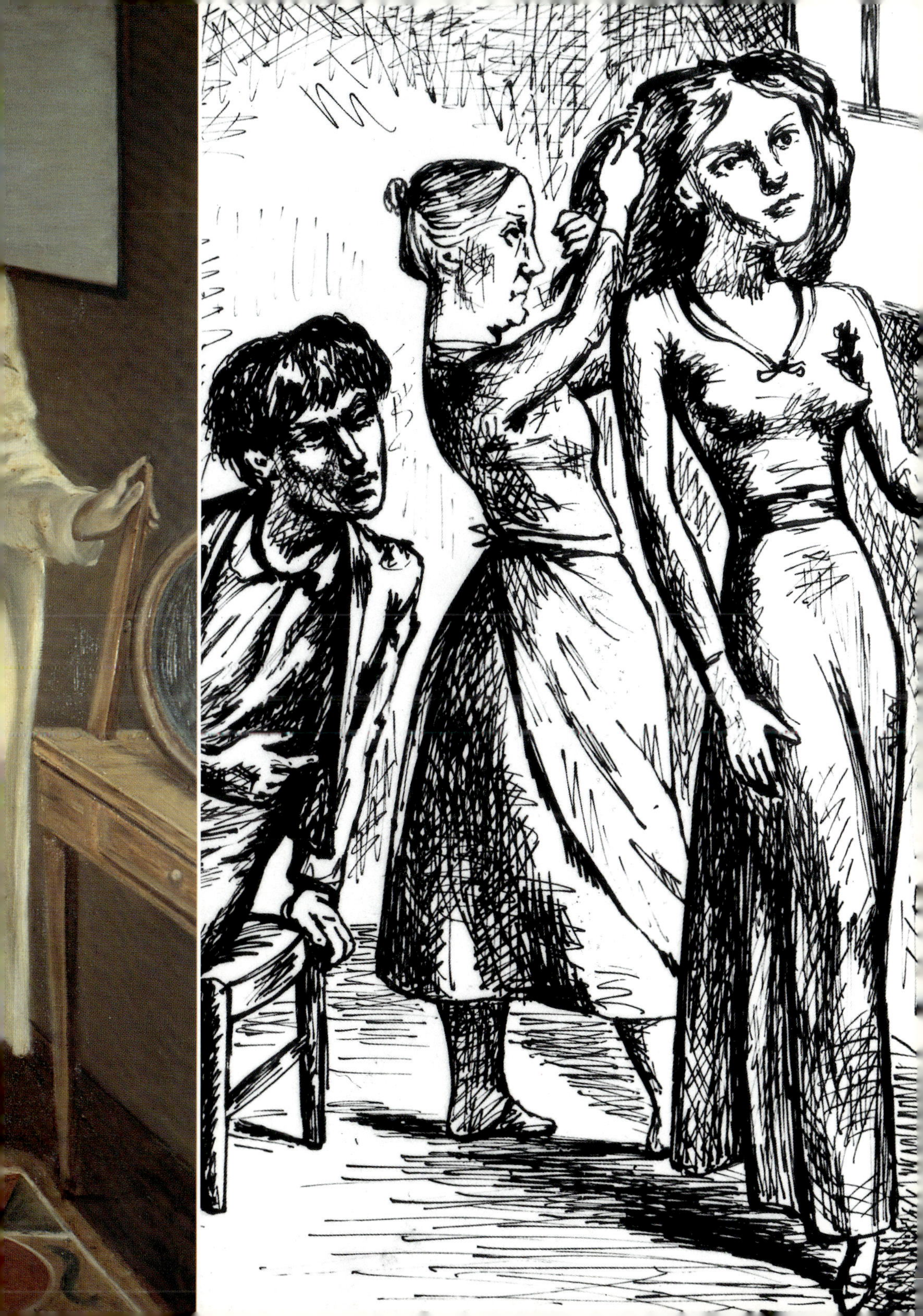

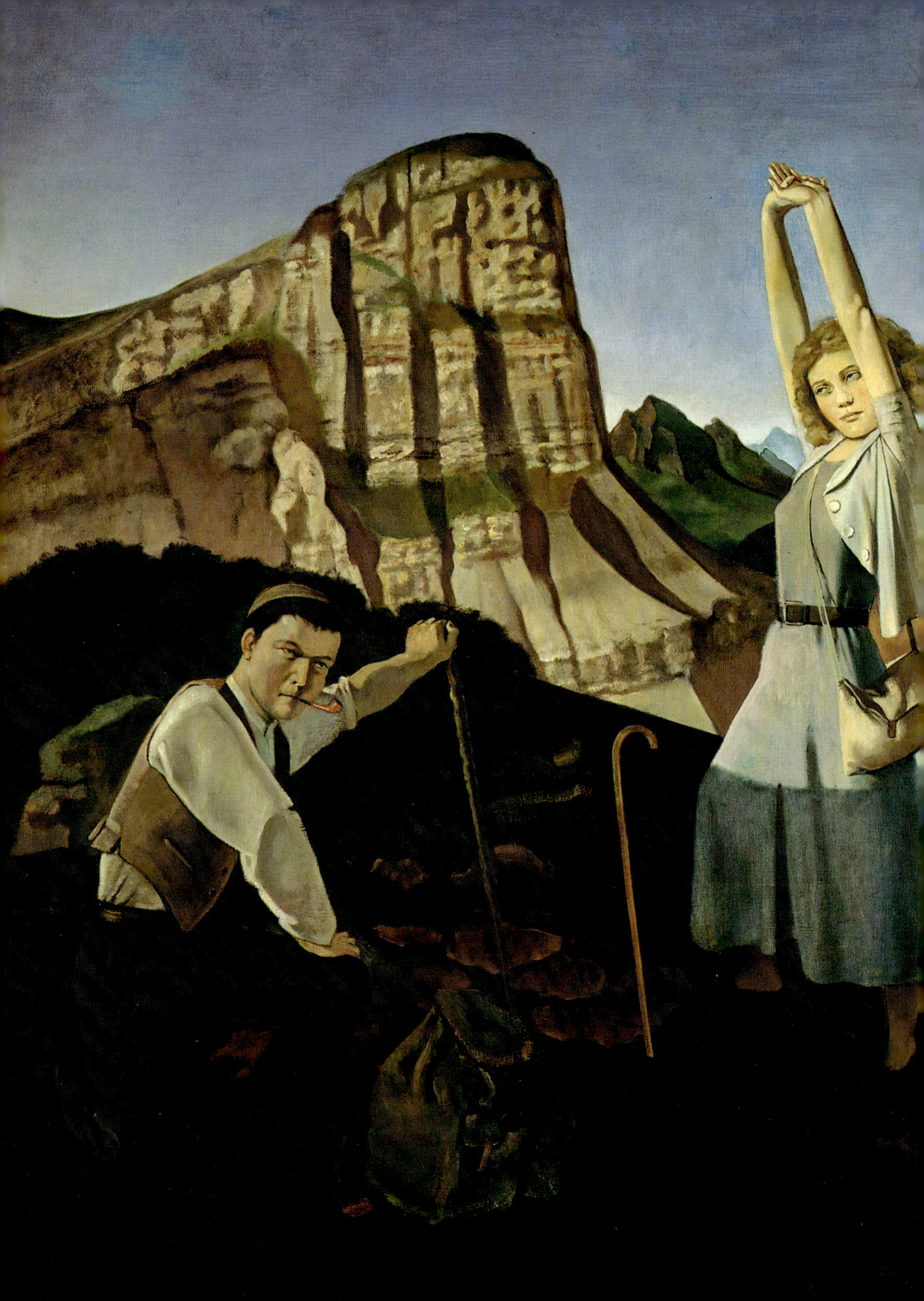

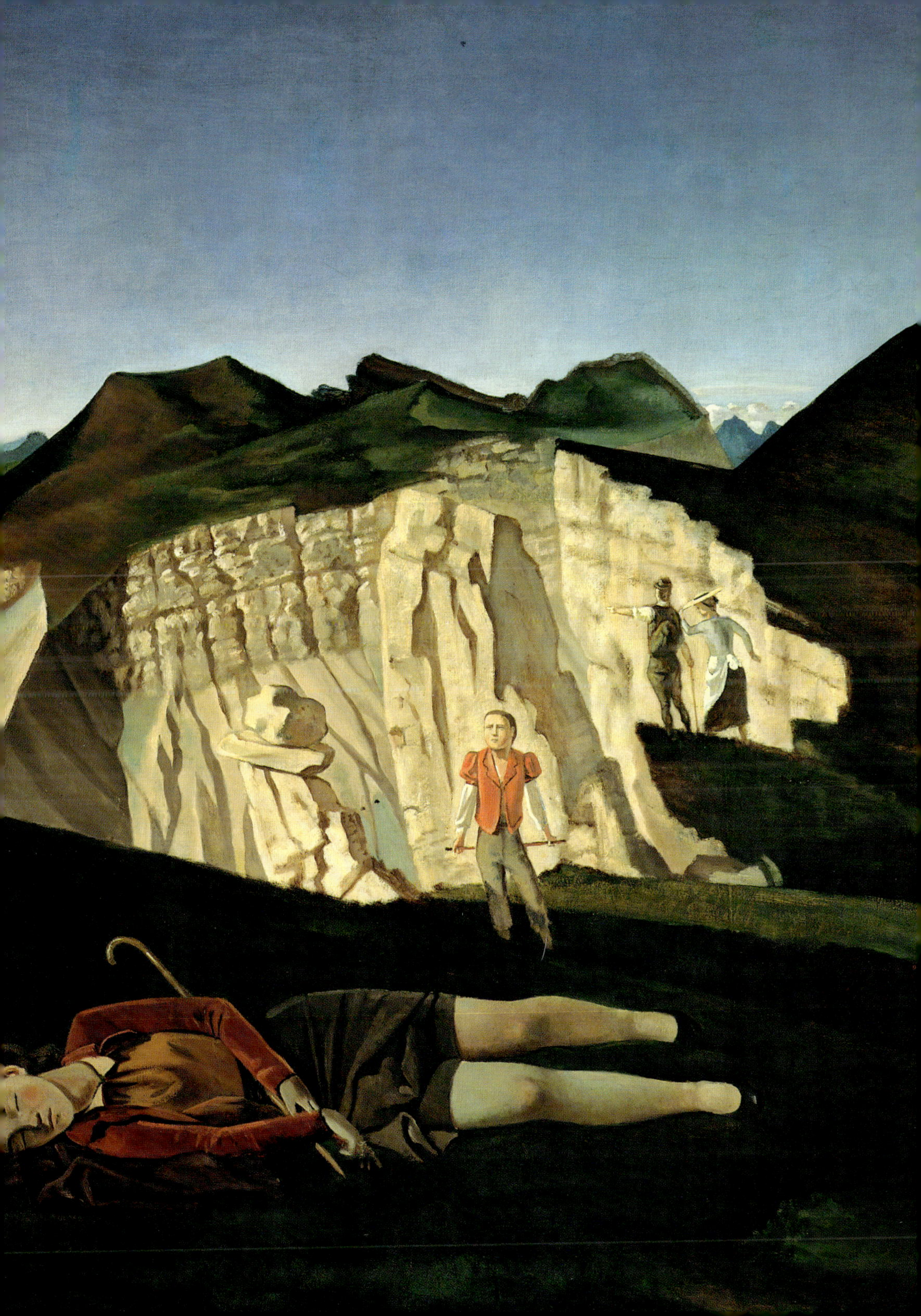

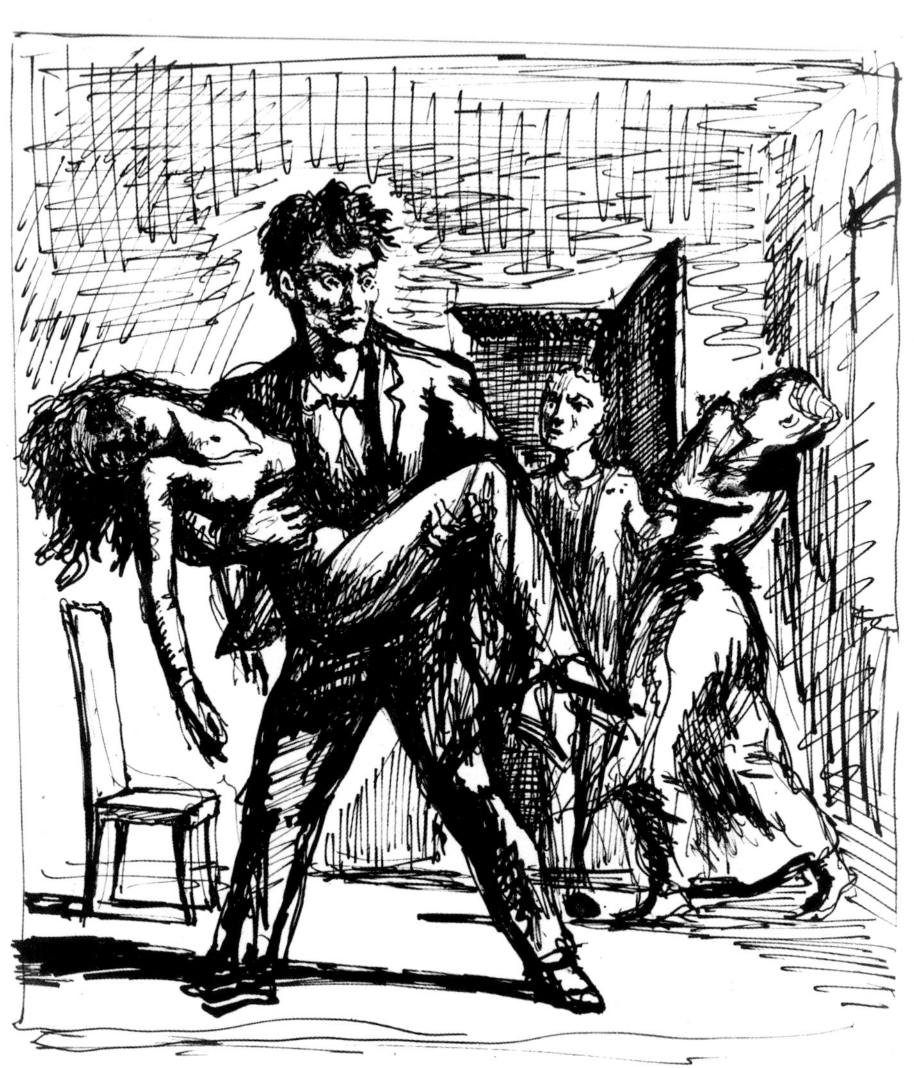

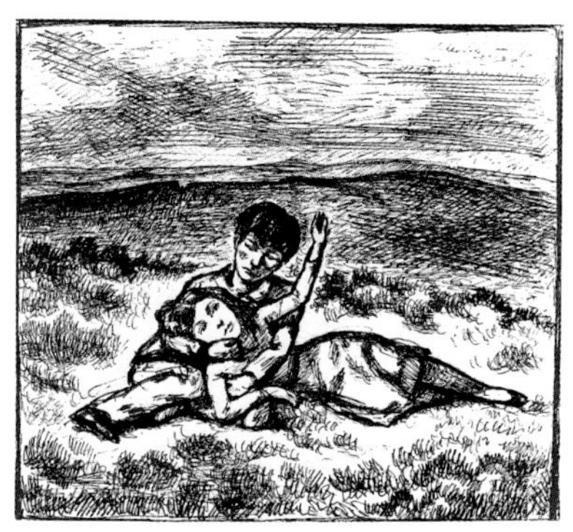

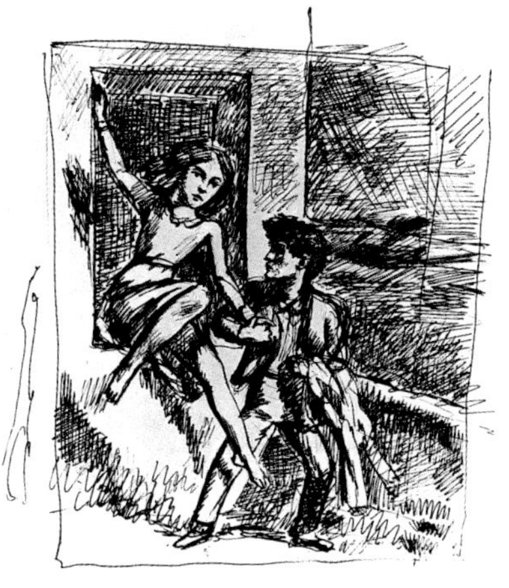

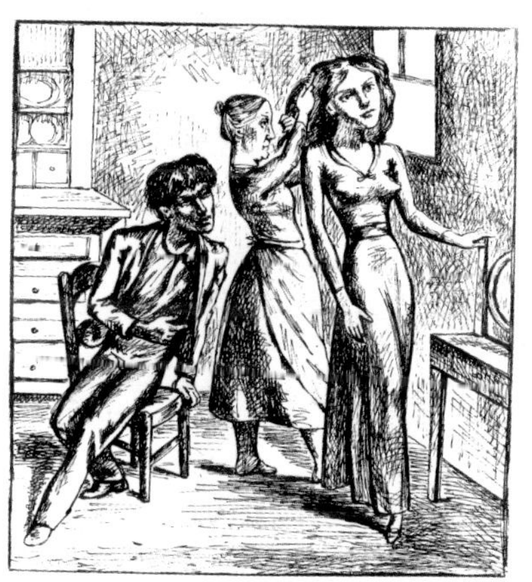

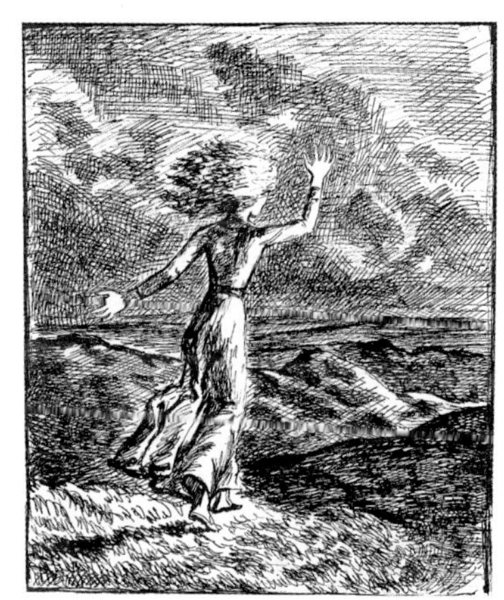

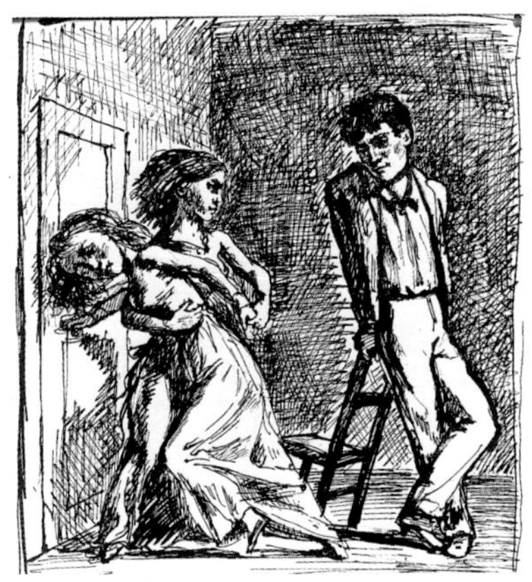

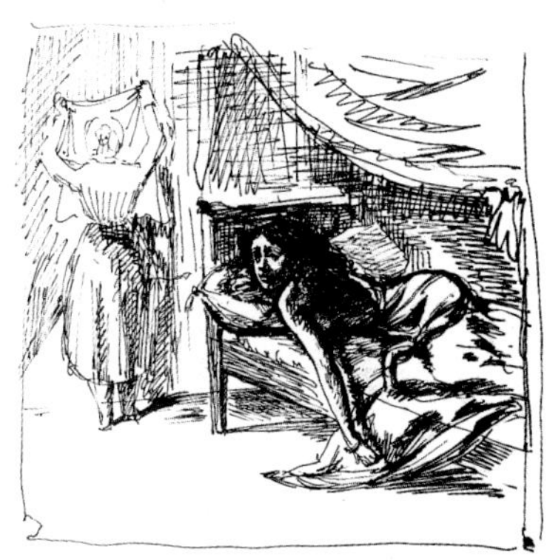

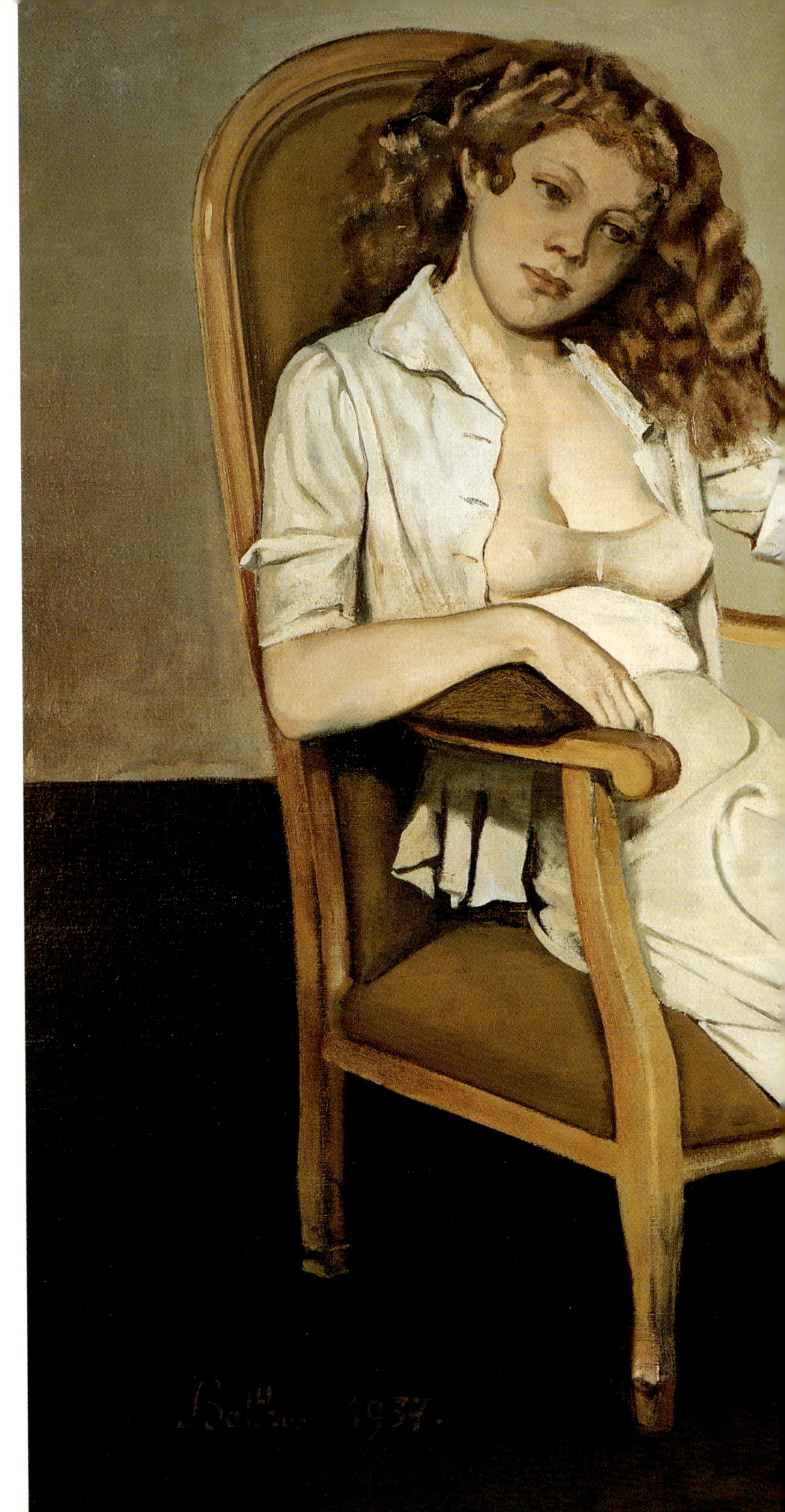
Balthus 1937.

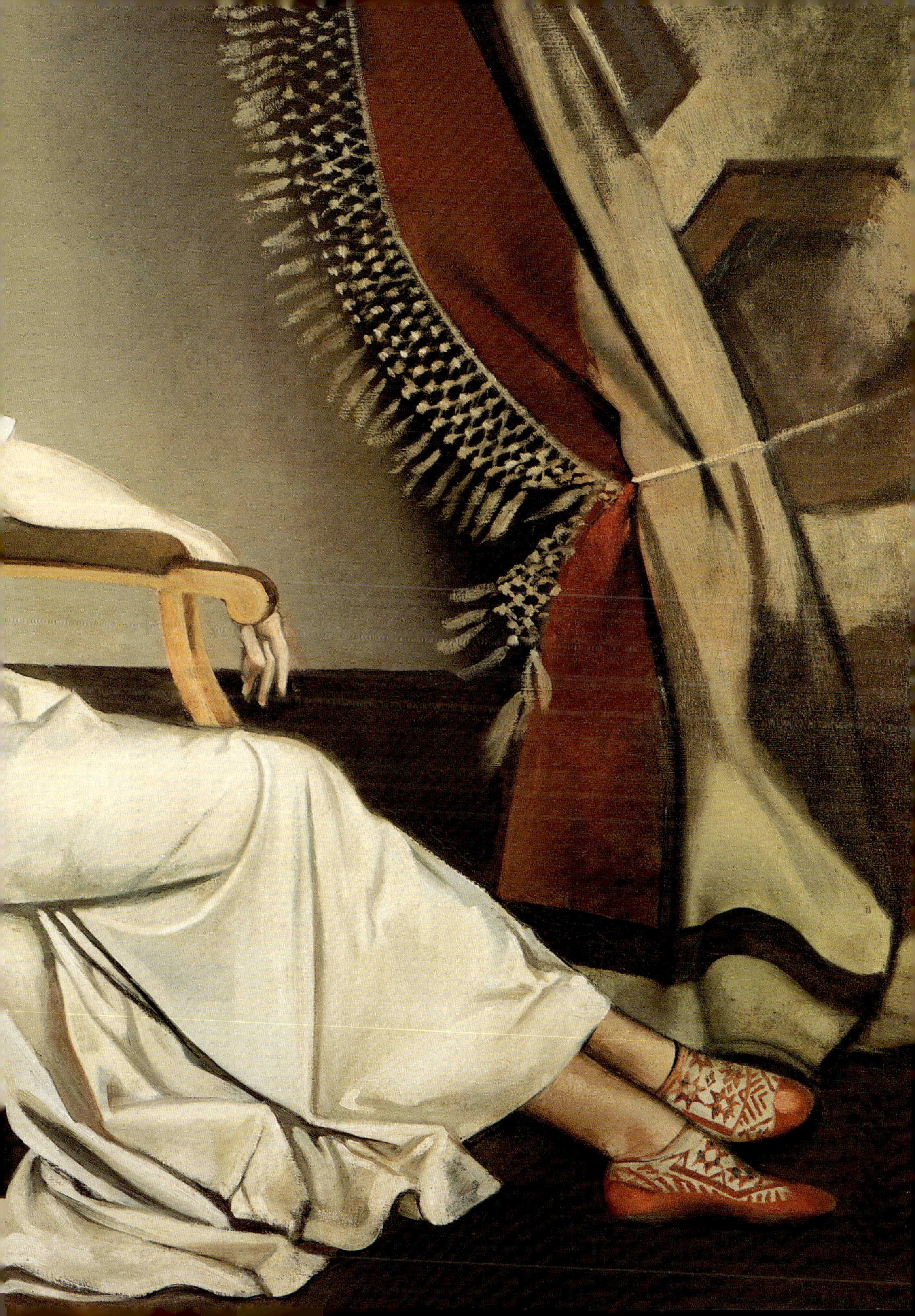

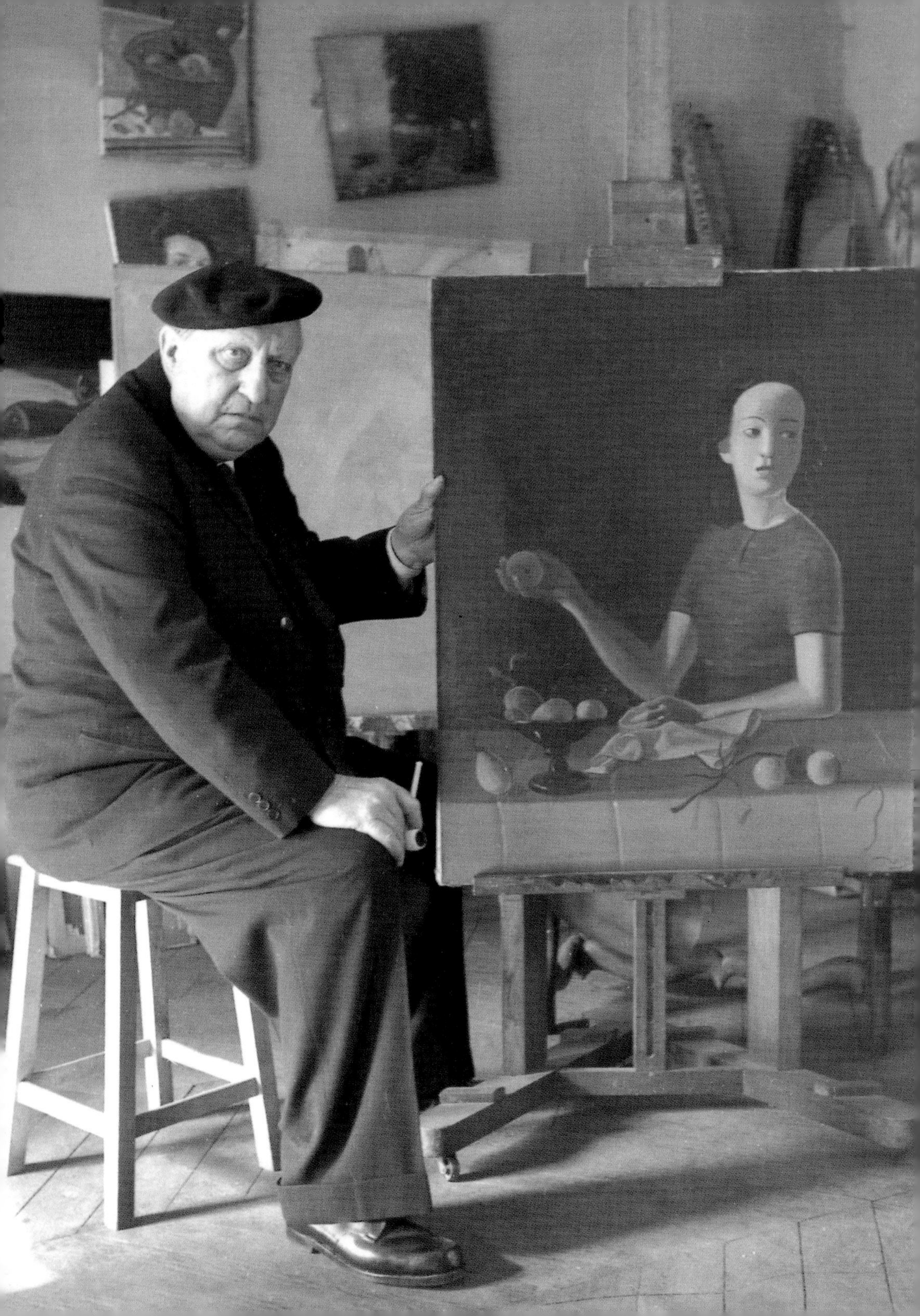

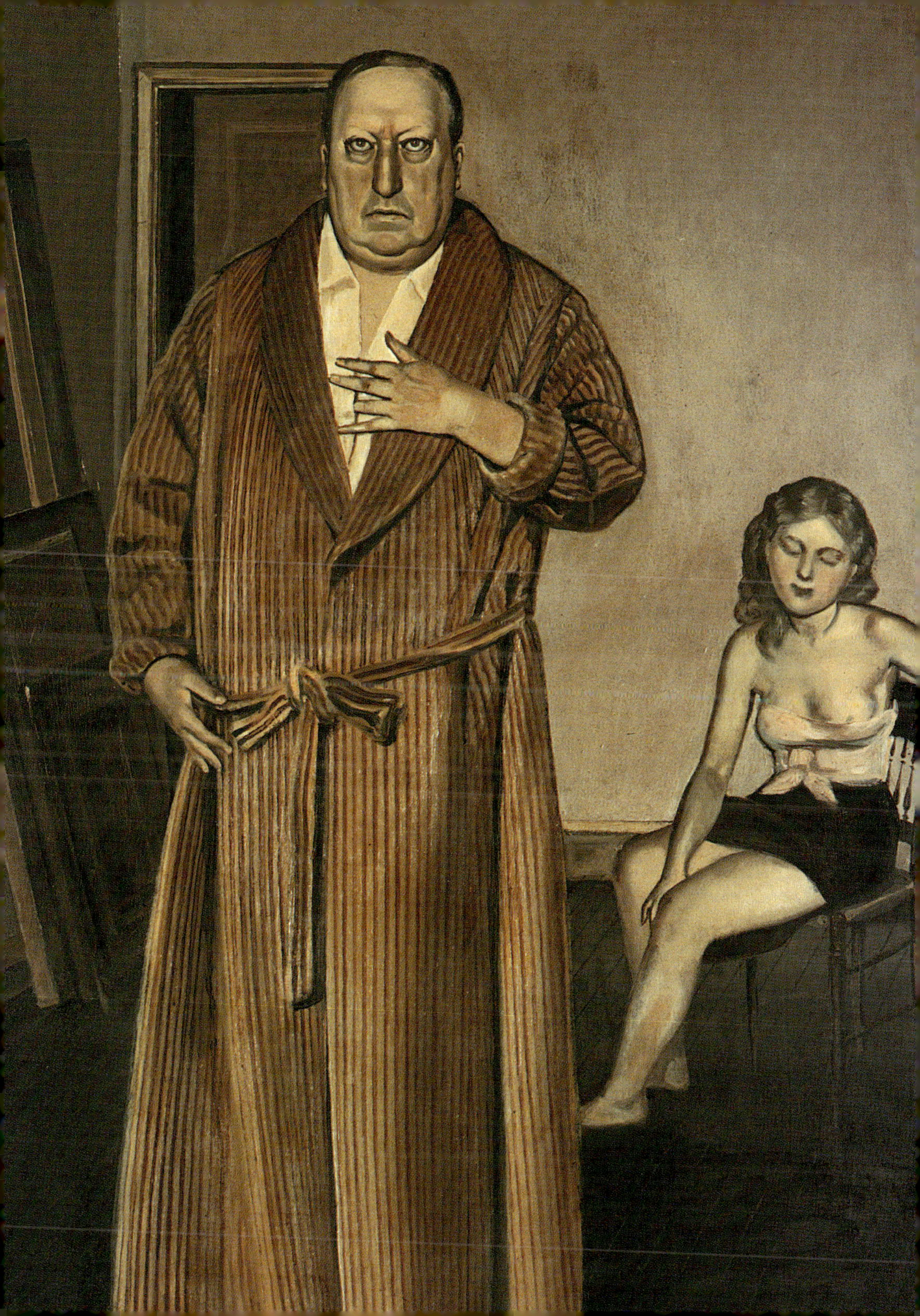

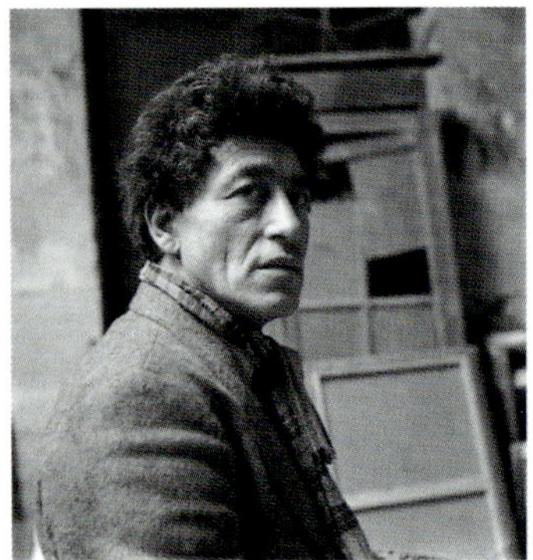

Alberto Giacometti in his studio
on rue Hippolyte-Maindron, Paris (1953).

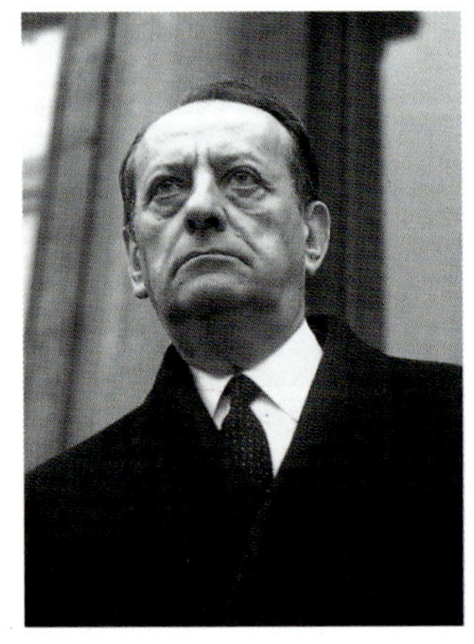

André Malraux (1958).

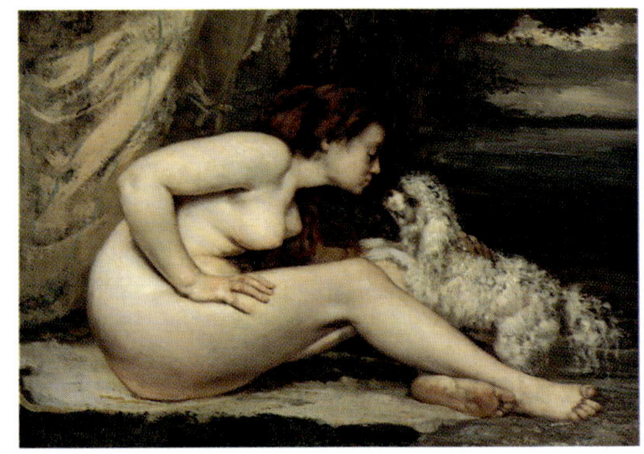

Nude with a Dog, Gustave Courbet,
1861–1862, oil on canvas ($25^{3/5}$" x 32").

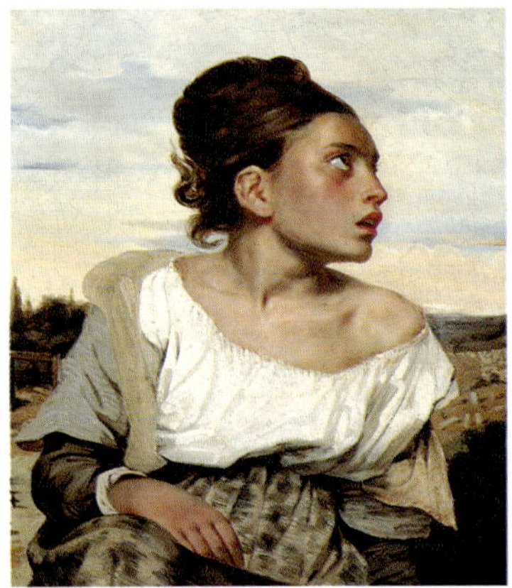

Orphan Girl at the Cemetery, Eugène Delacroix,
1823, oil on canvas ($25^{4/5}$" x $21^{3/8}$").

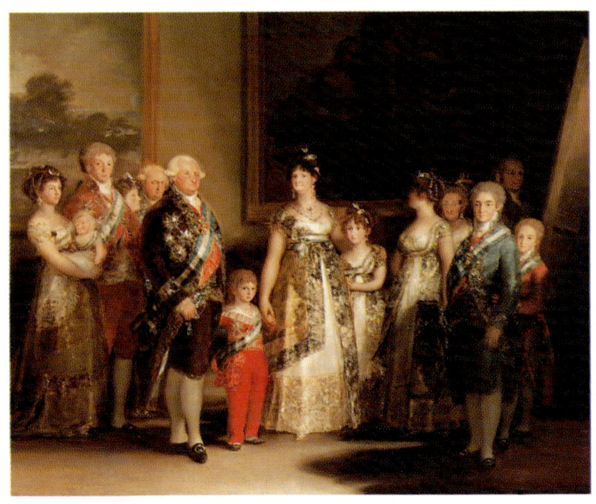

Charles IV and his Family, Francisco de Goya,
1800, oil on canvas (110" x 93").

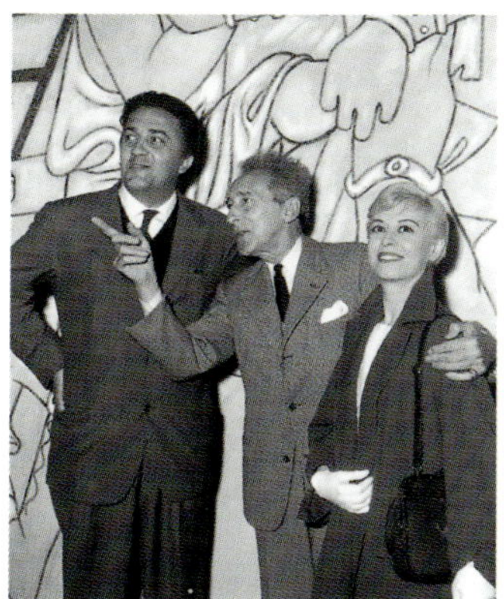

Federico Fellini, Jean Cocteau
and Giulietta Masina (1957).

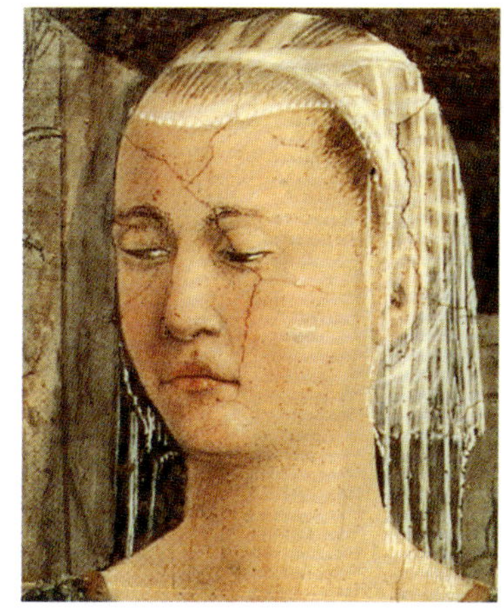

Detail of a fresco by Piero della Francesca
in the Church of San Francesco,
Arezzo, Italy, circa 1460.

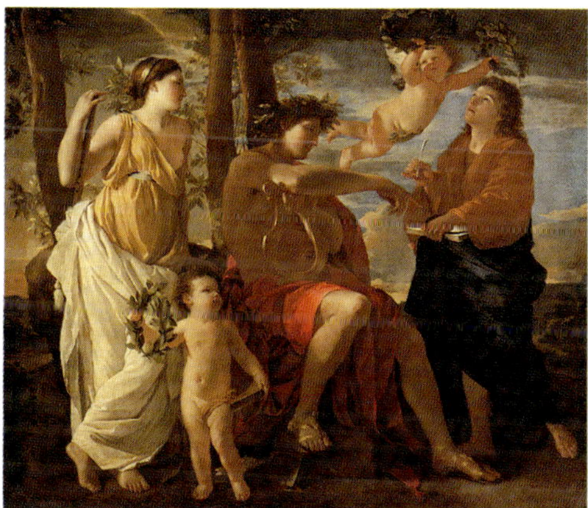

The Inspiration of the Poet, Nicolas Poussin (1595–1665),
n.d., oil on canvas (71″ x 84″).

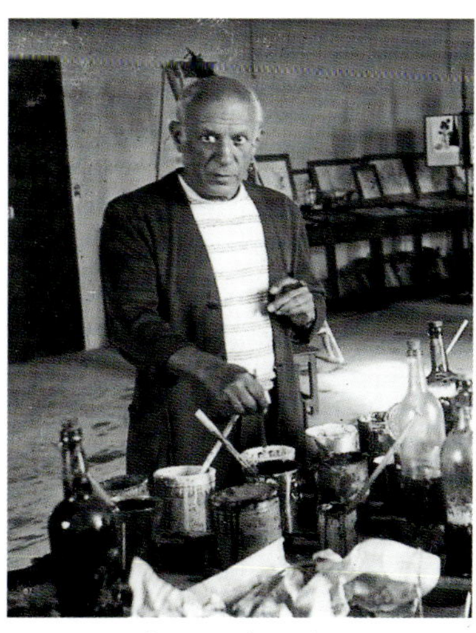

Picasso in his studio
in Antibes, France (1946).

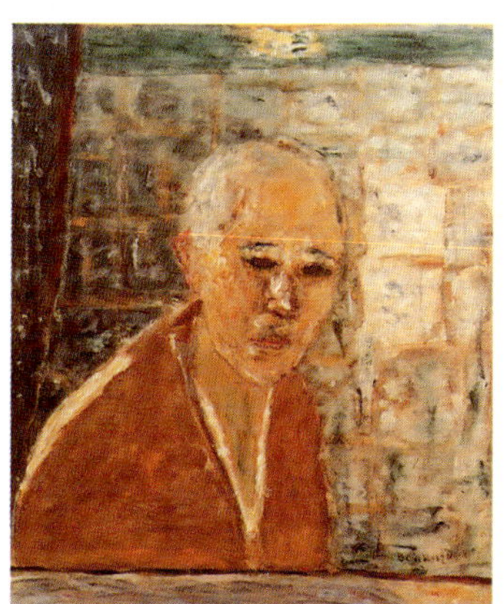

Self-portrait, Pierre Bonnard,
1945, oil on canvas (23 1/2″ x 18″).

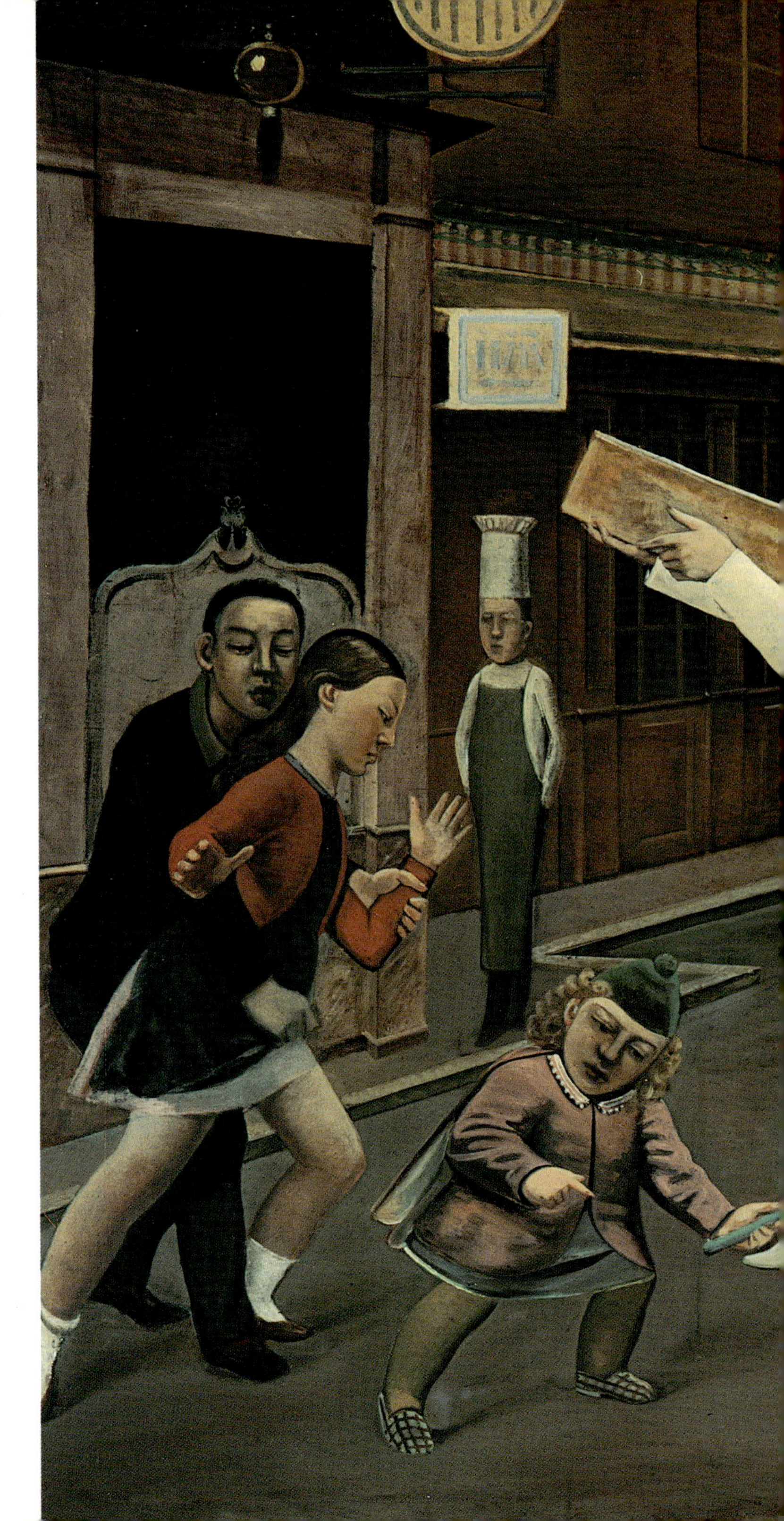

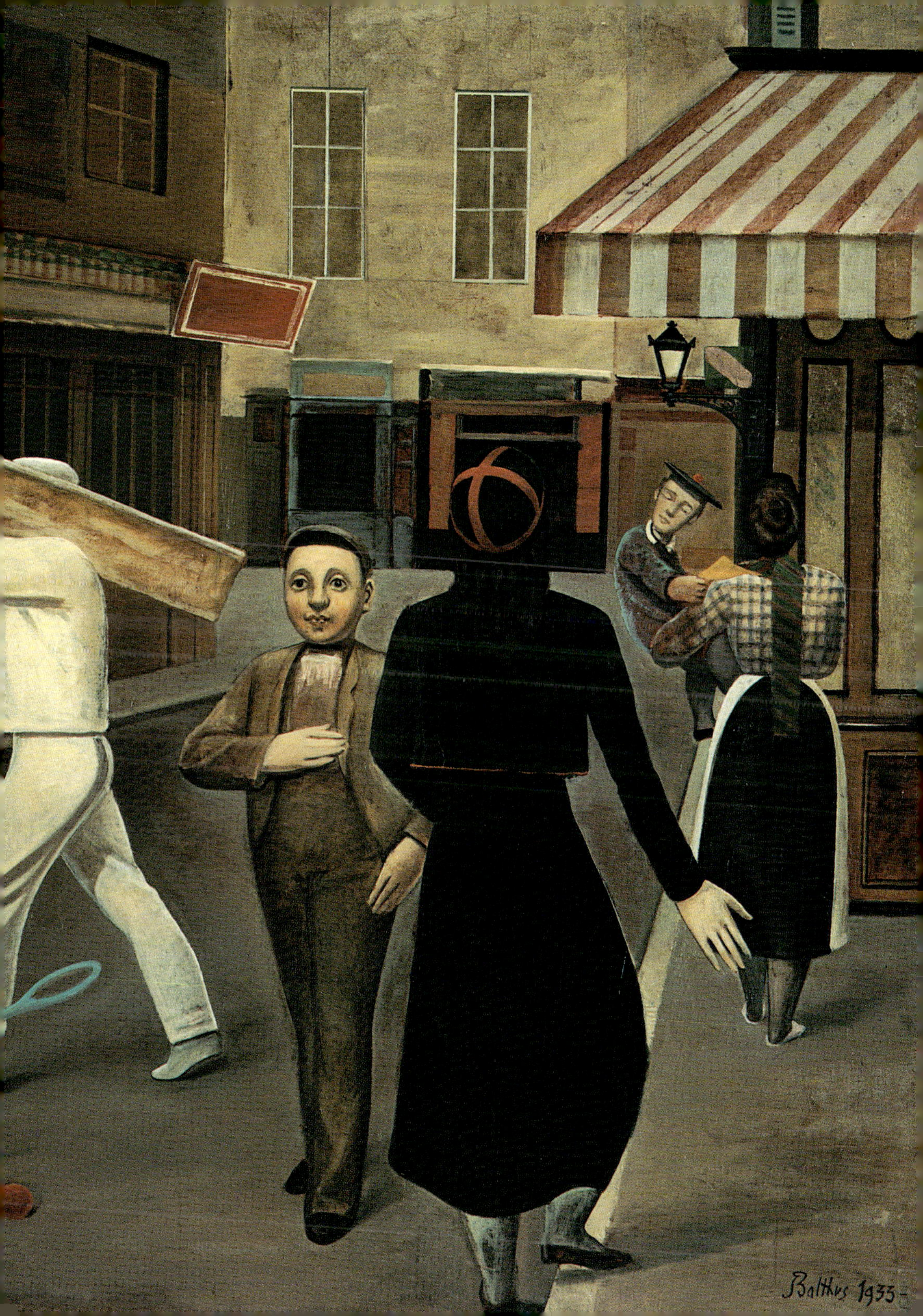
Balthus 1933

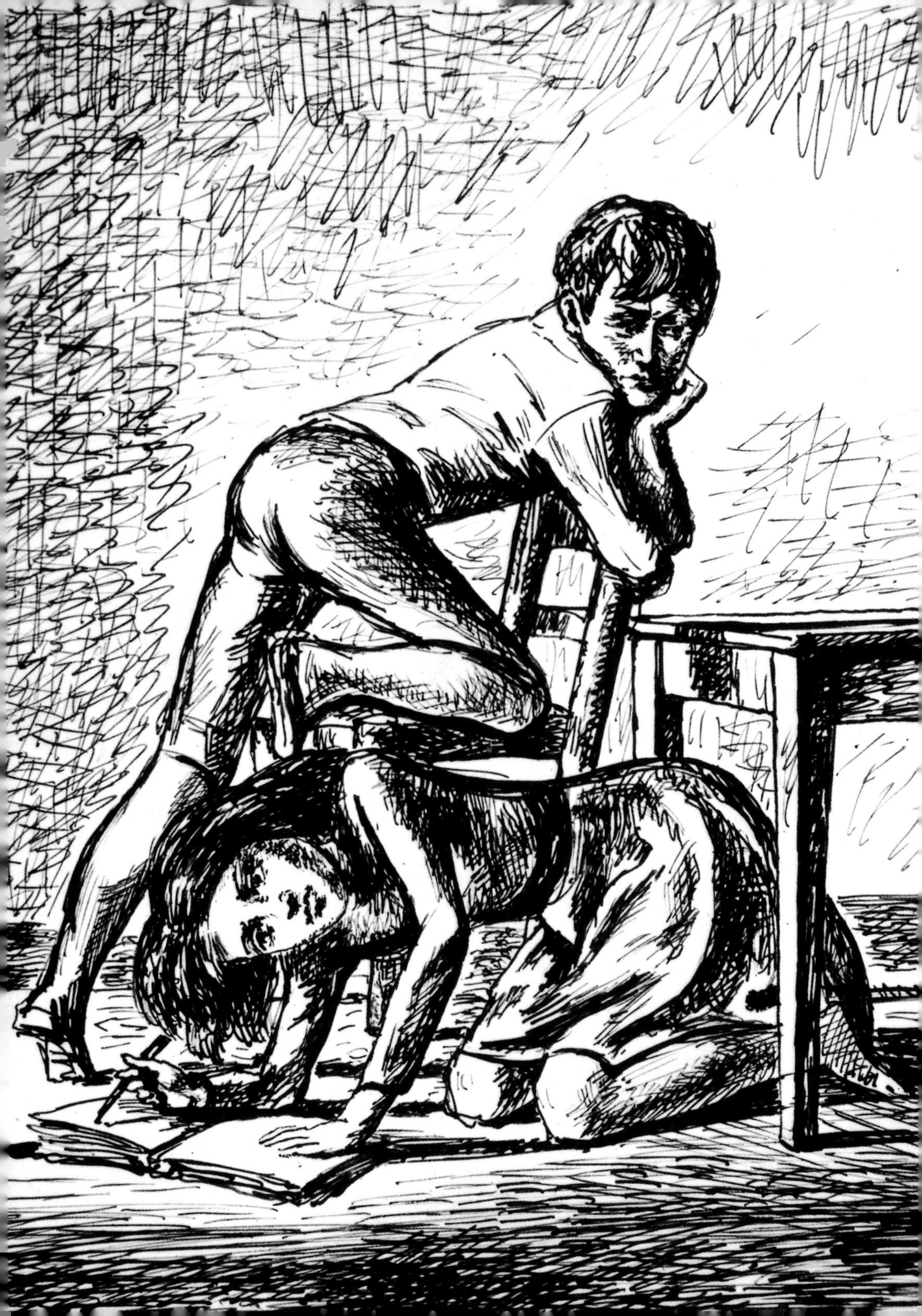

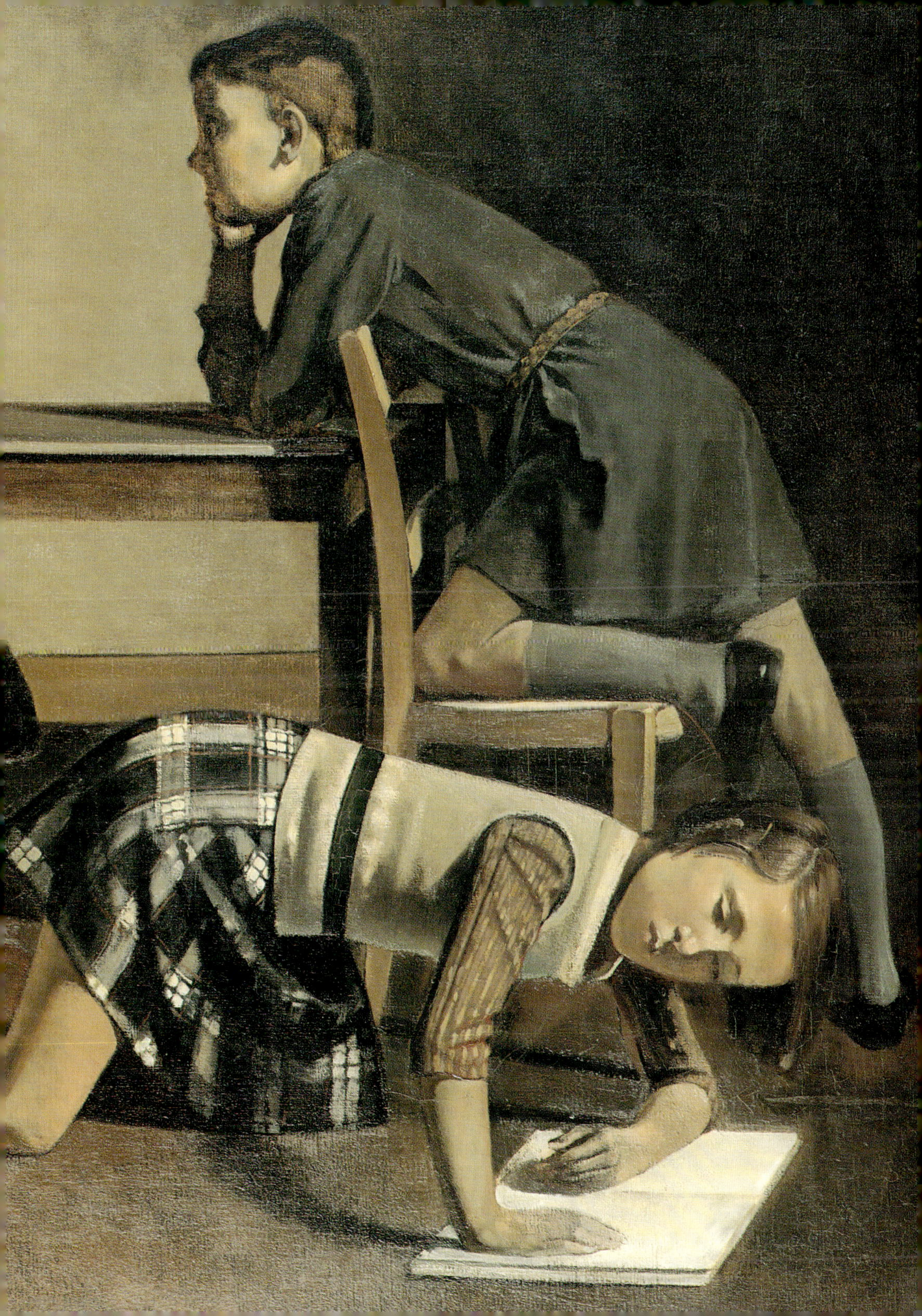

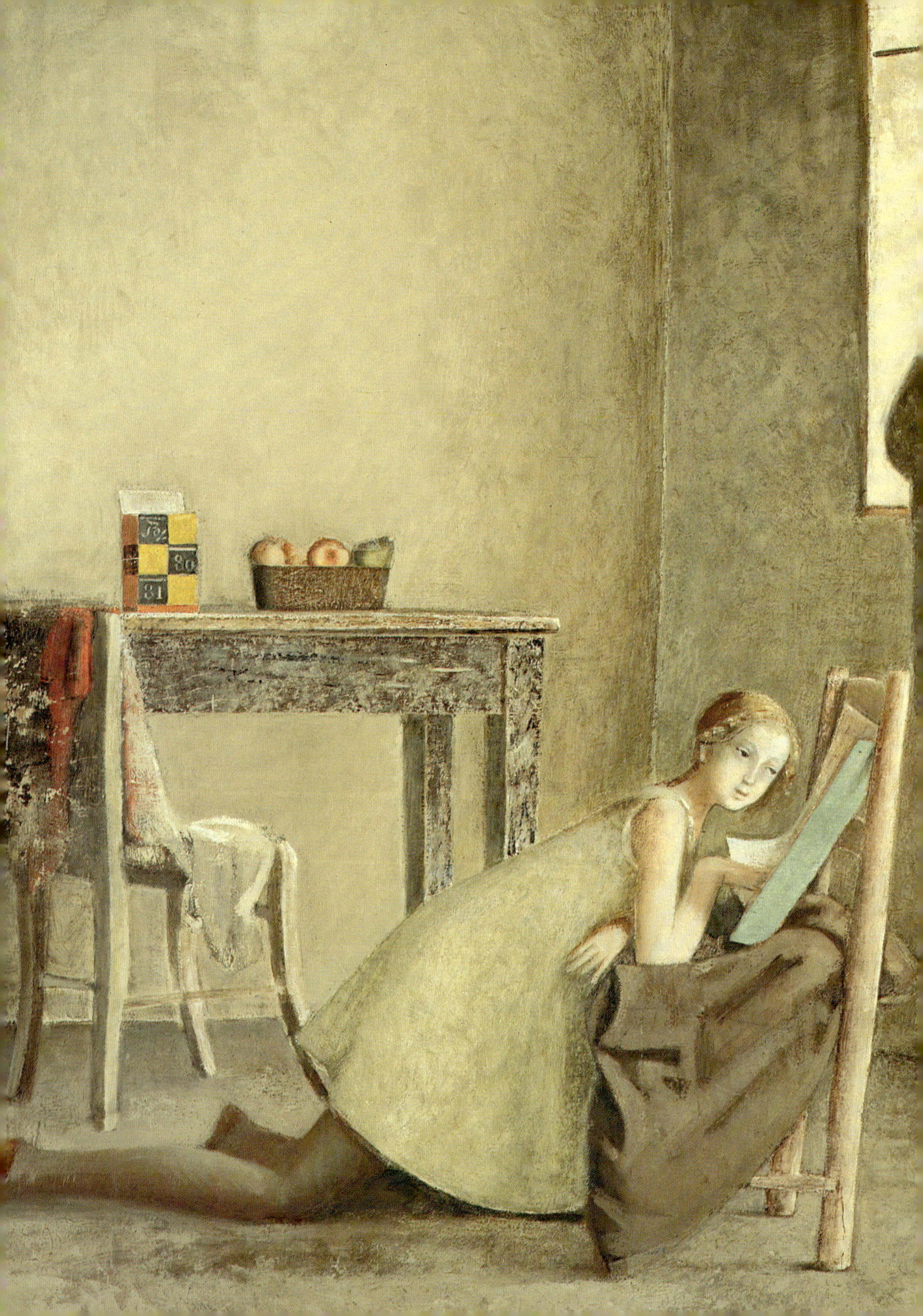

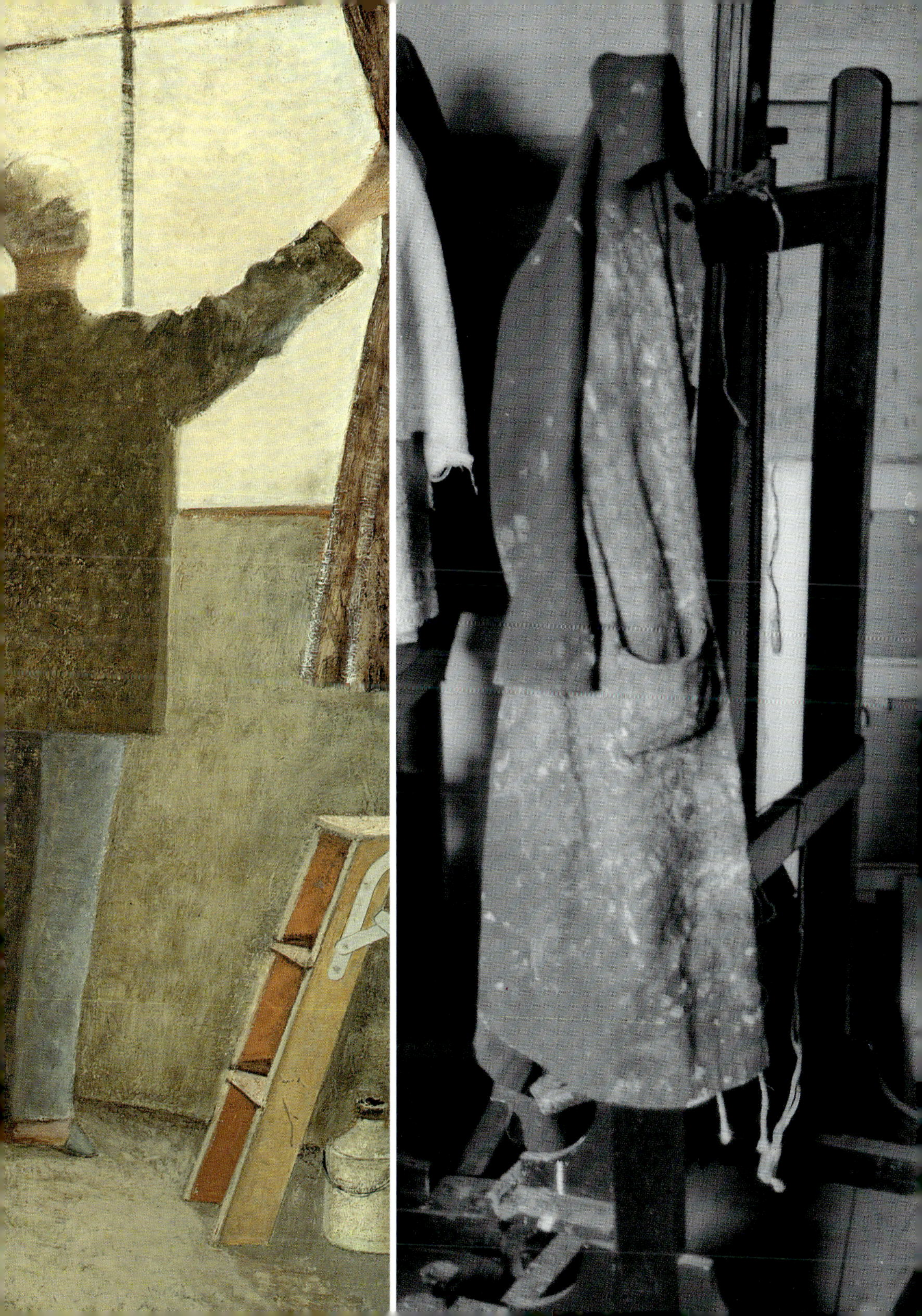

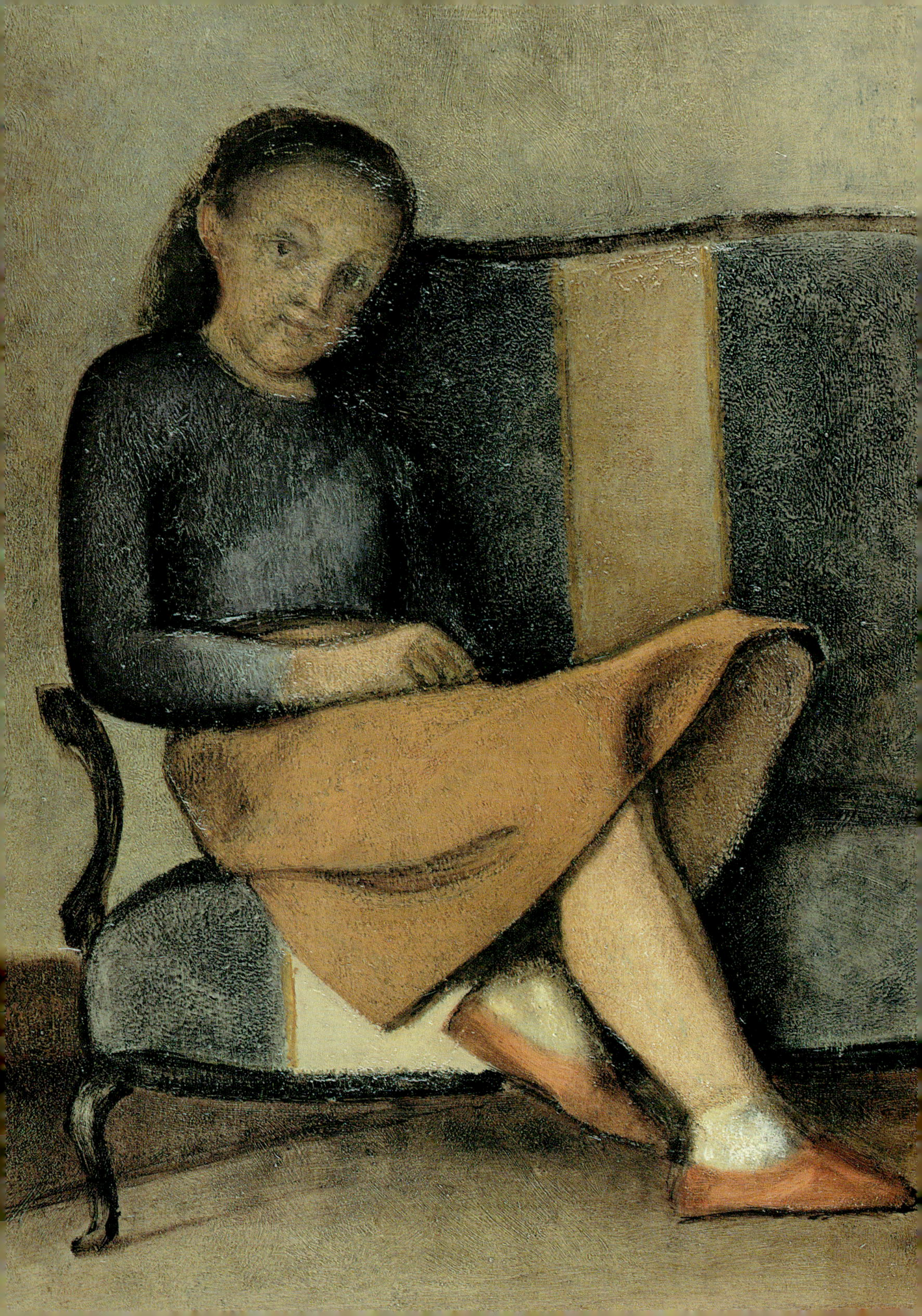

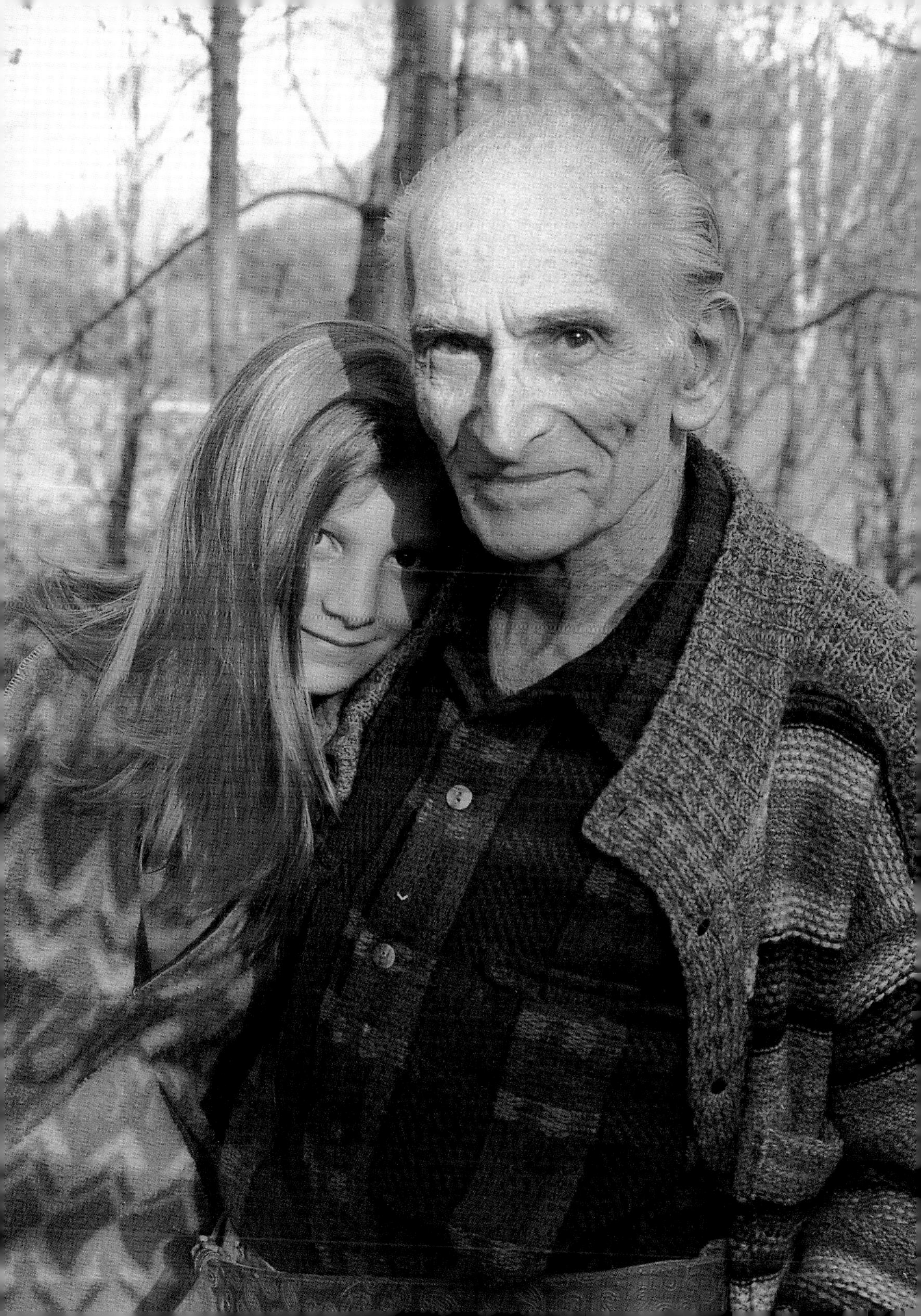

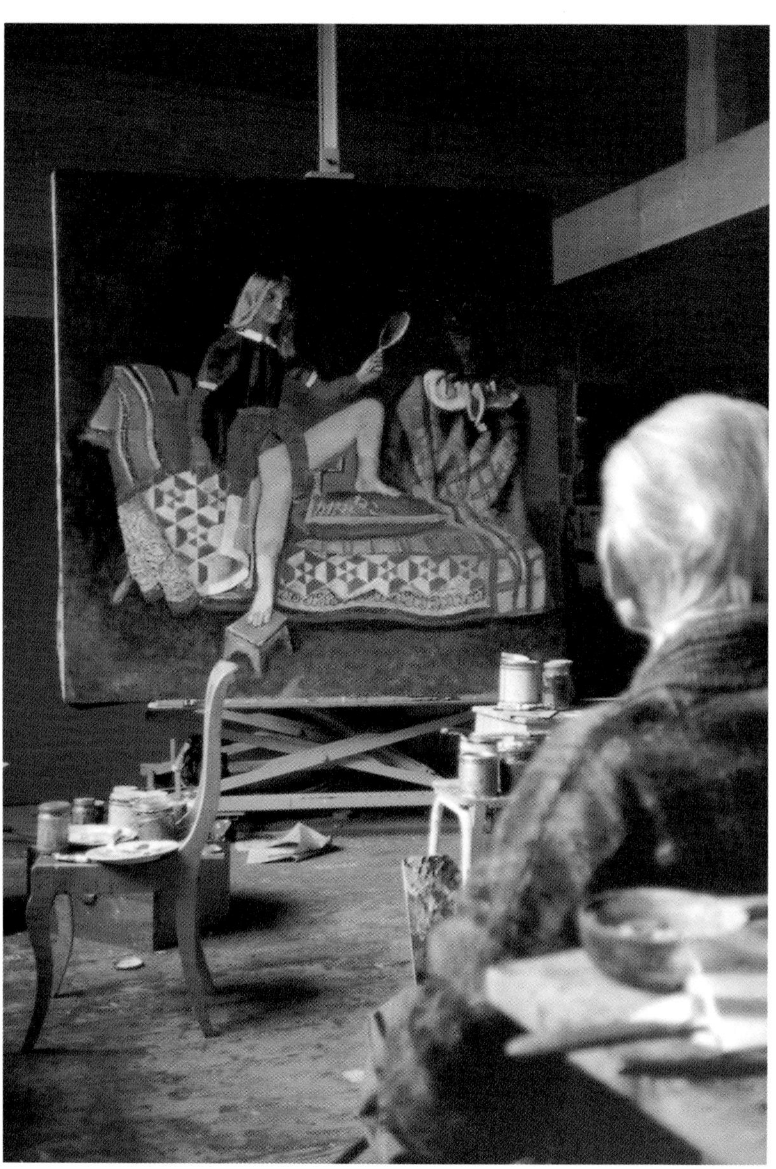

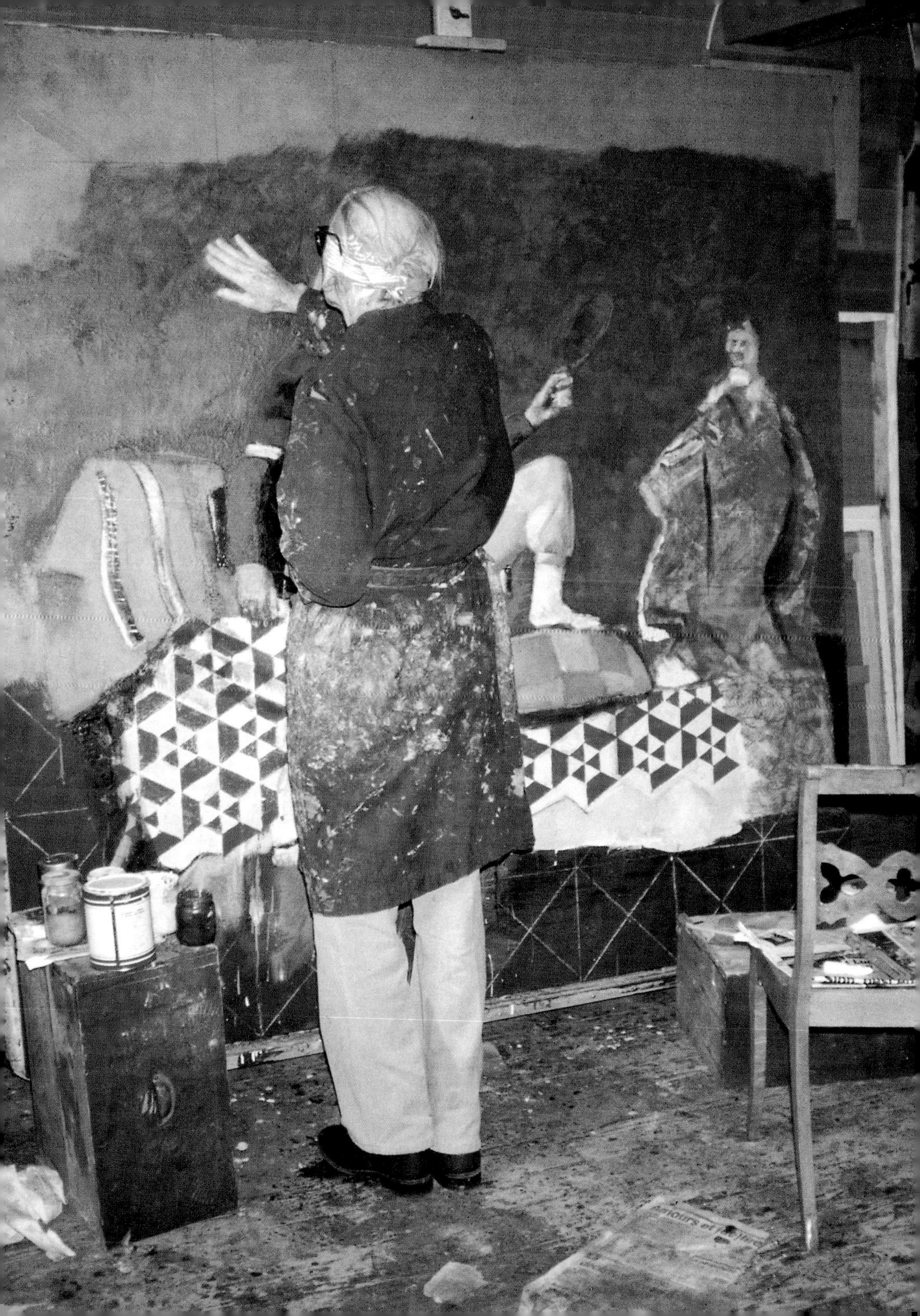

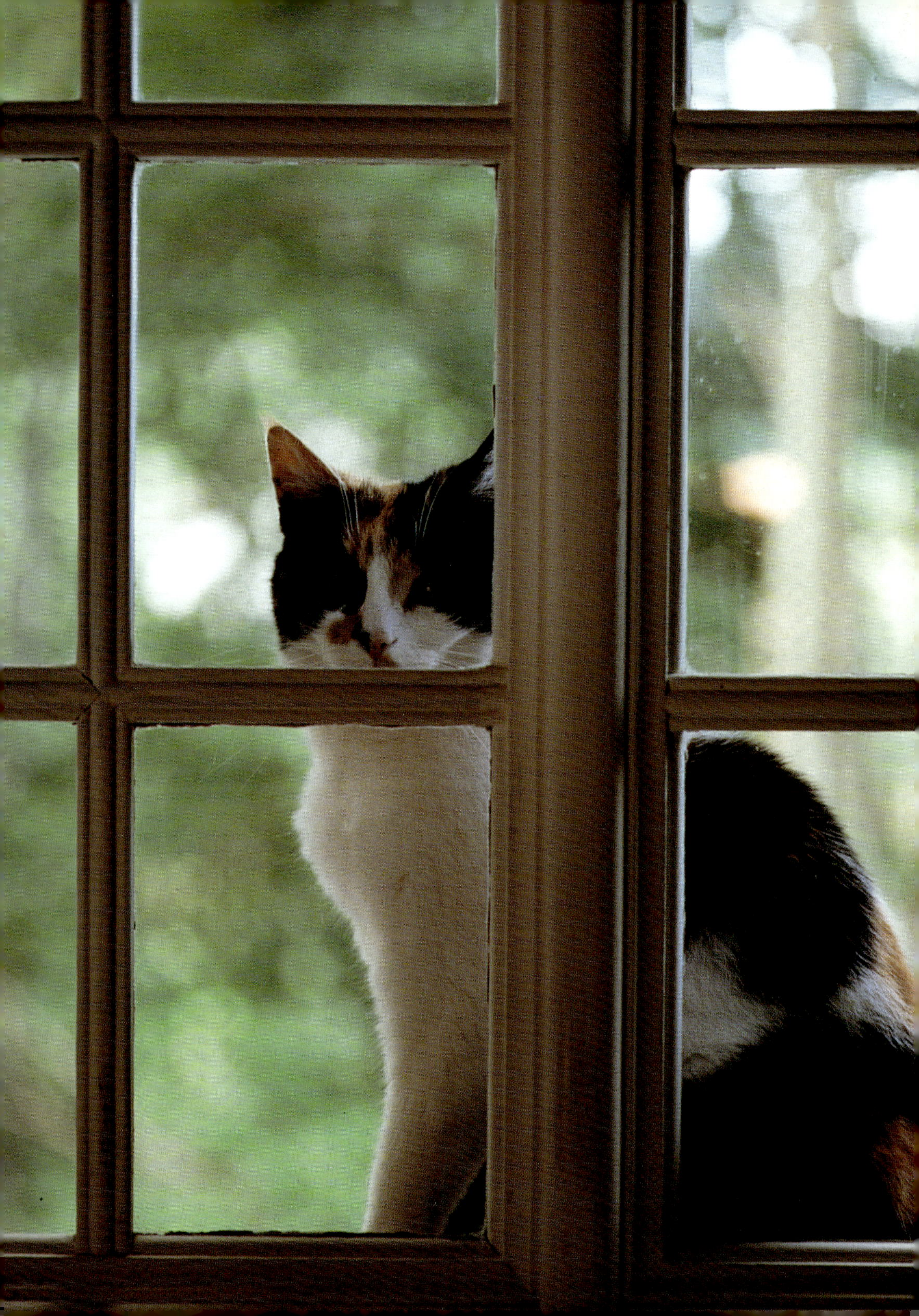

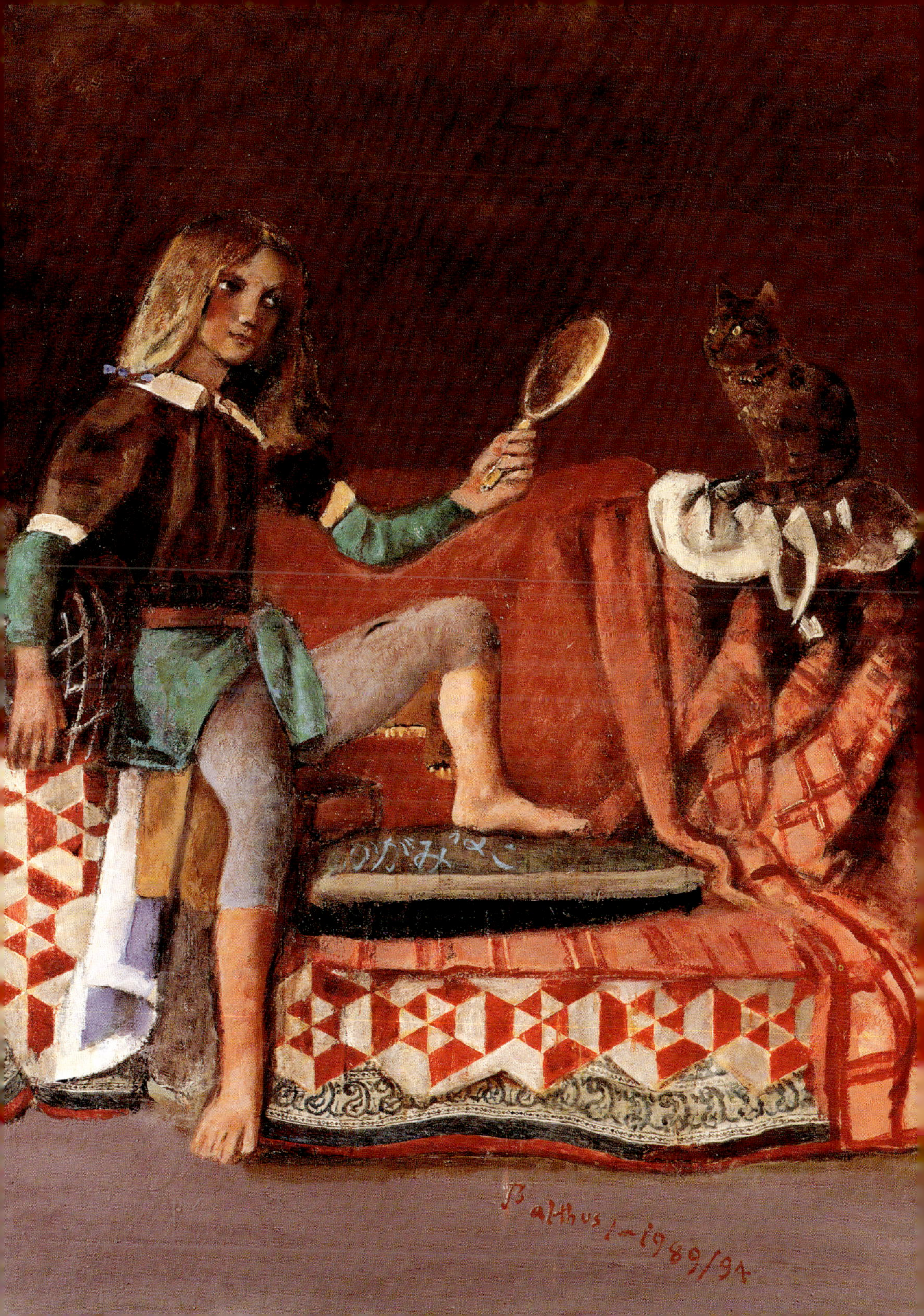
Balthus 1989/94

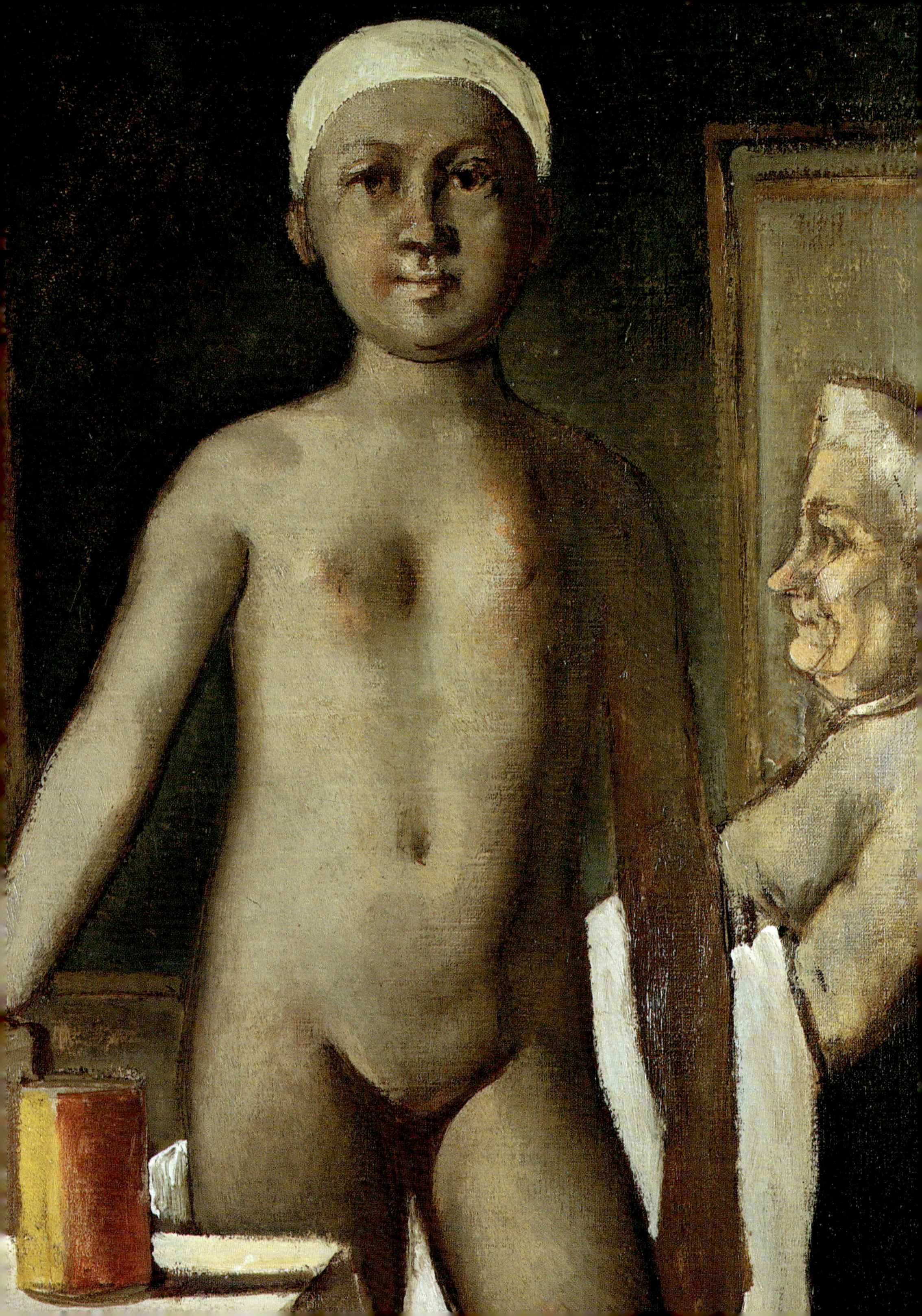

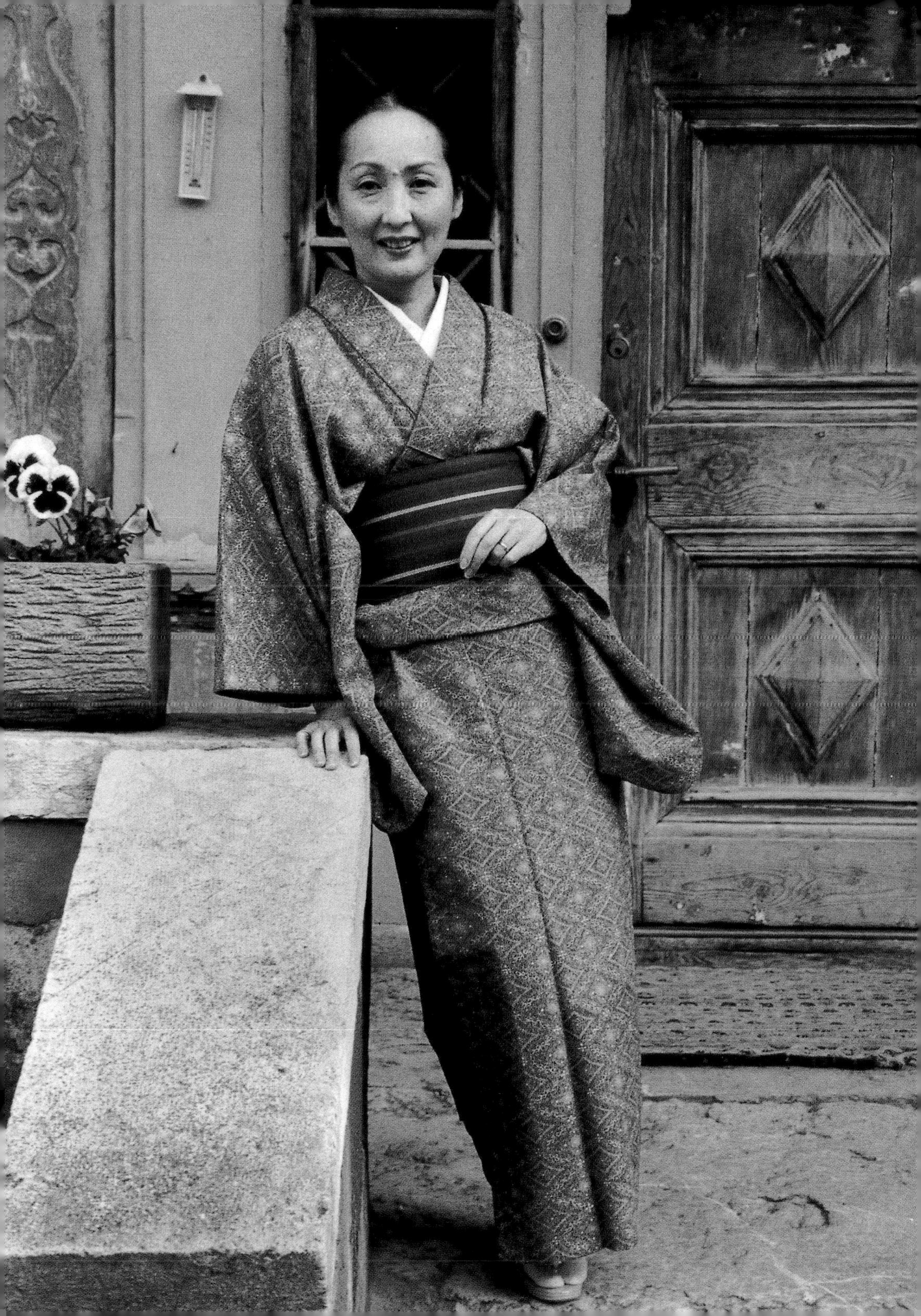

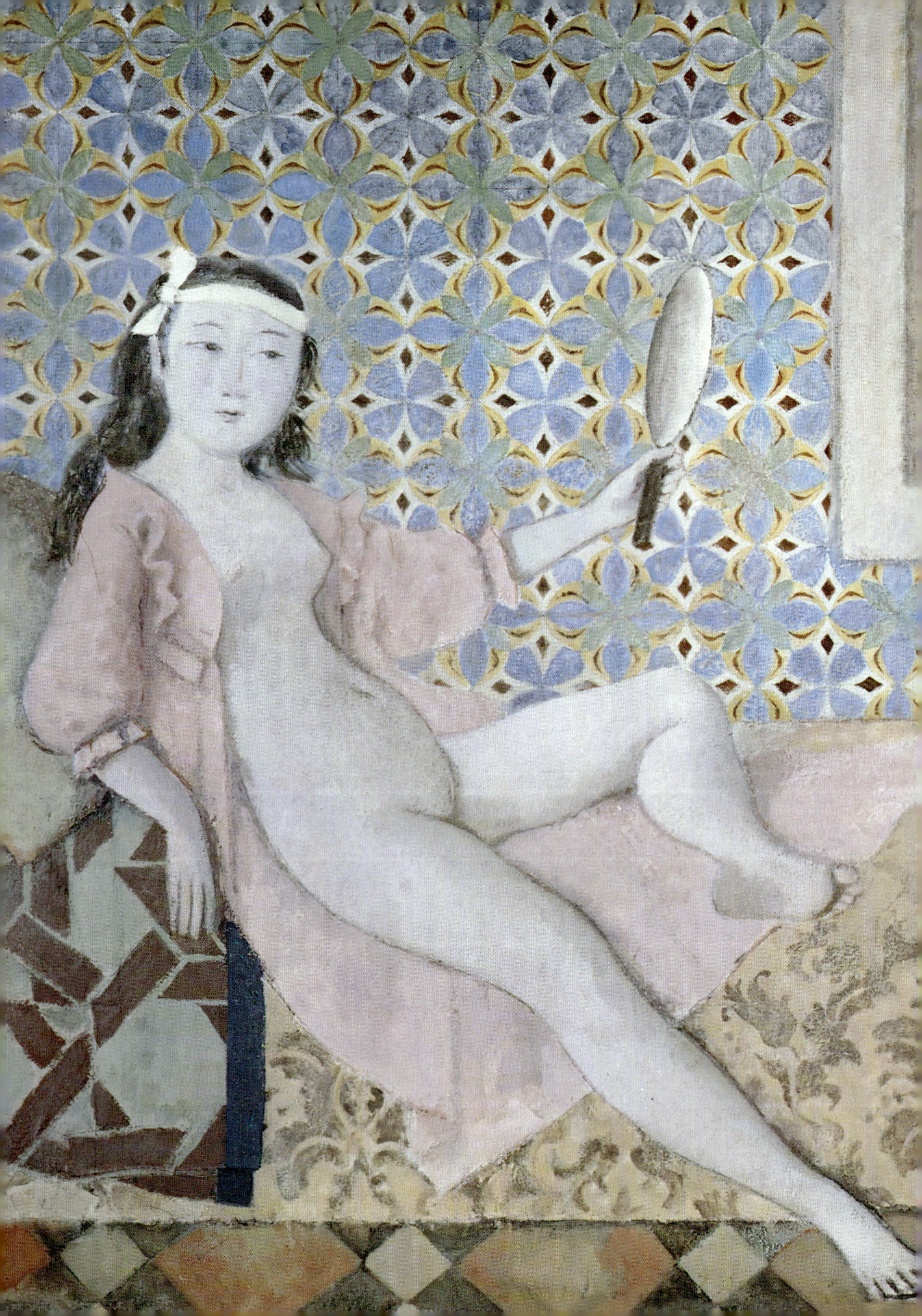

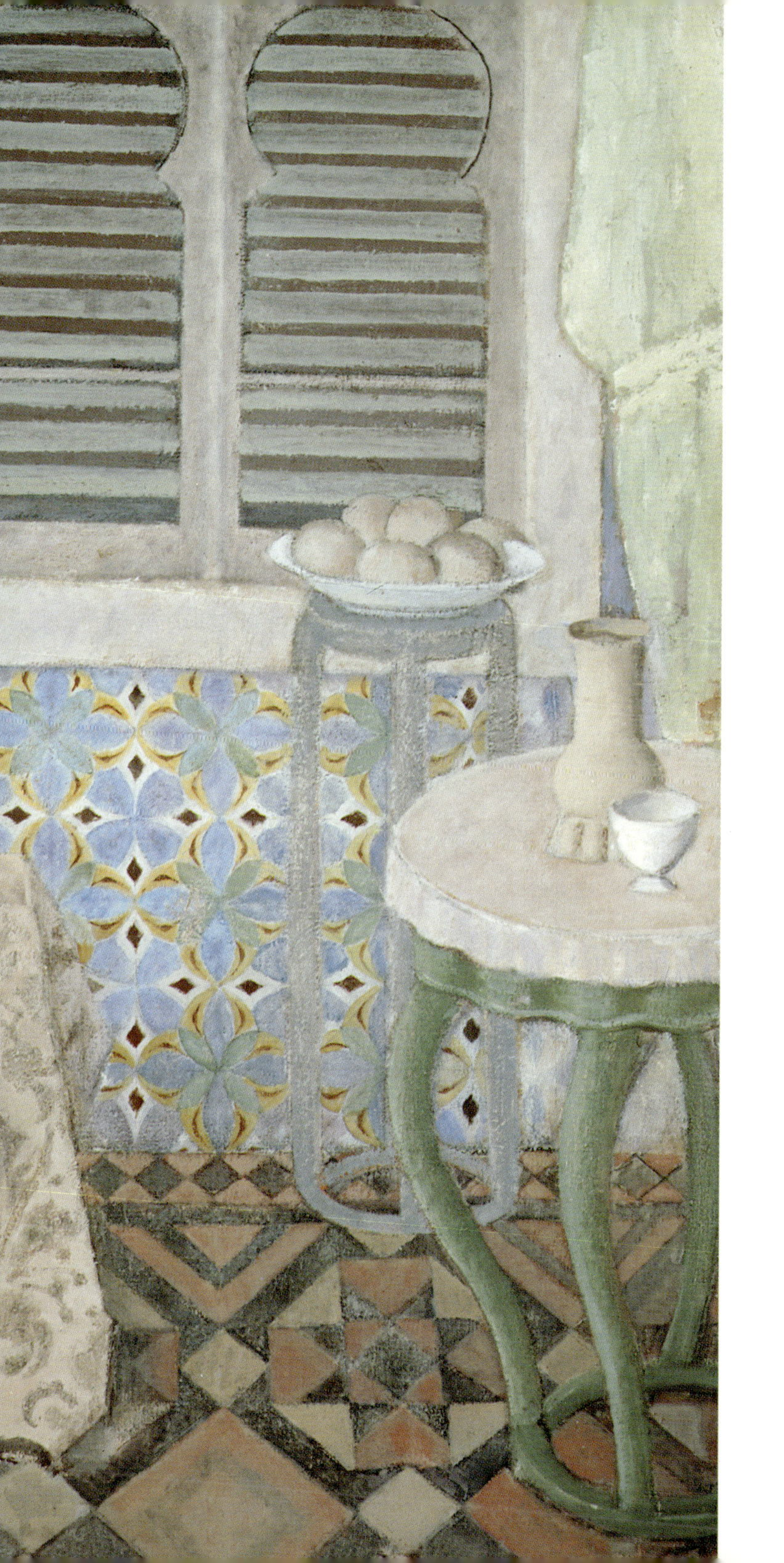

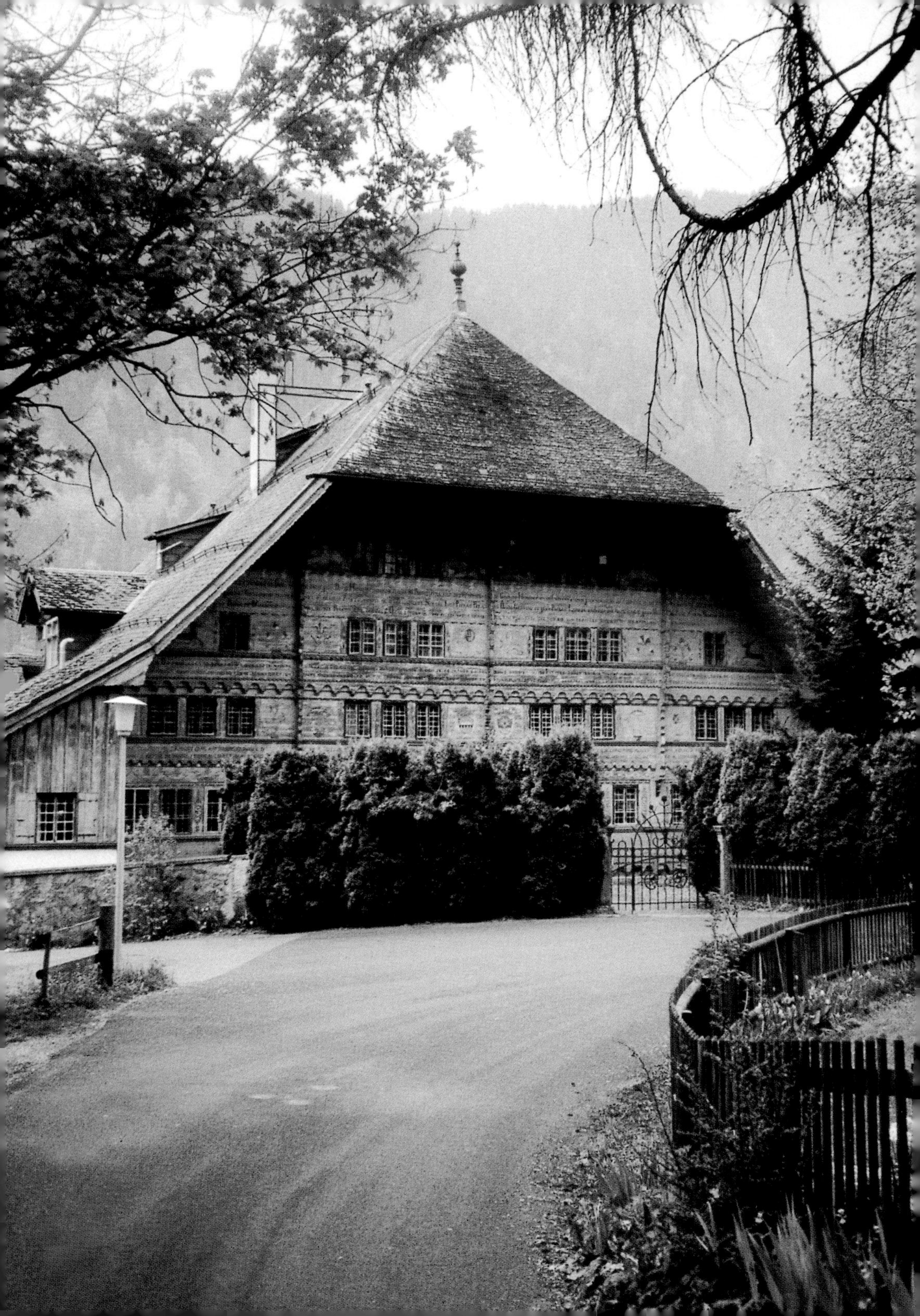

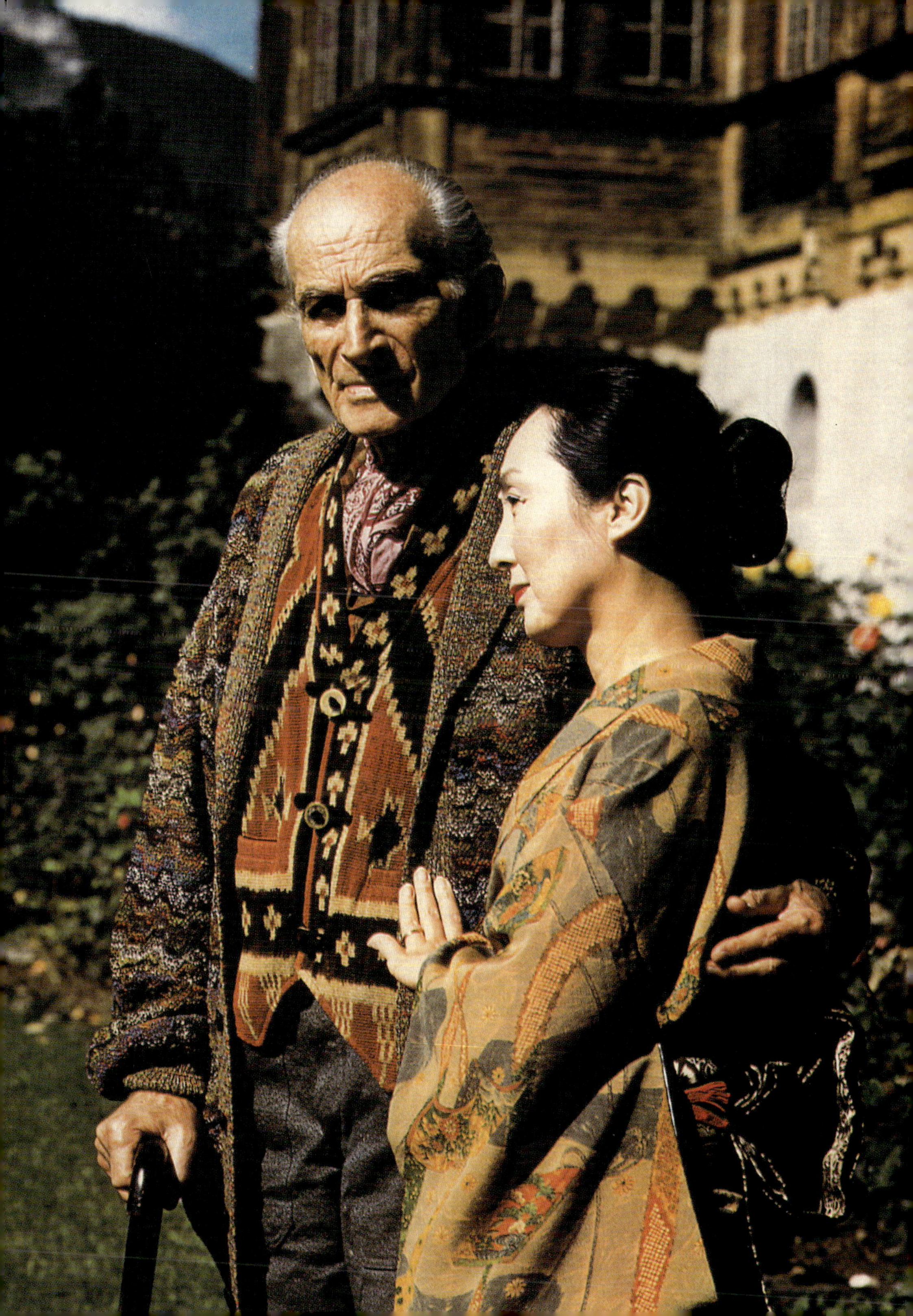

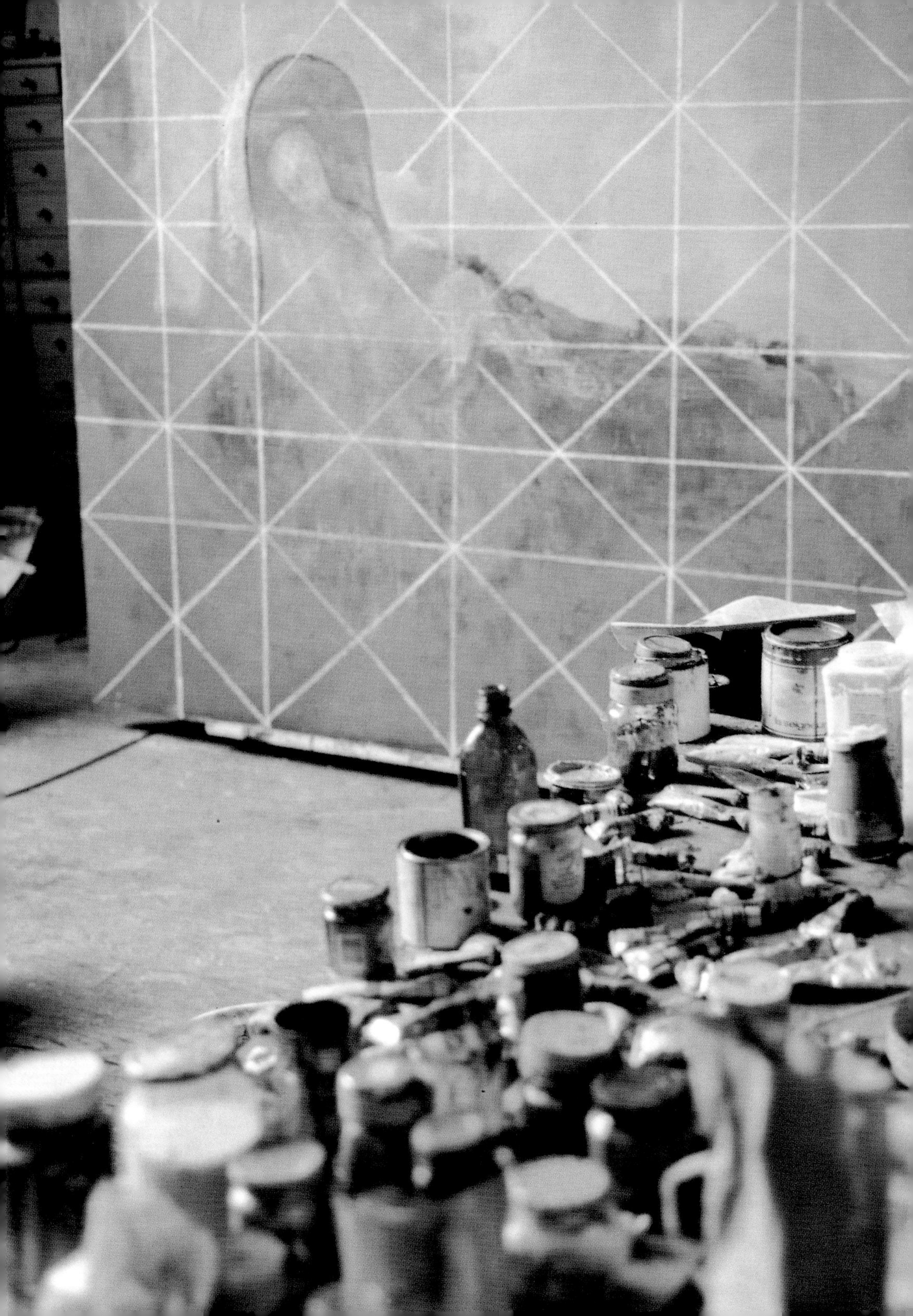

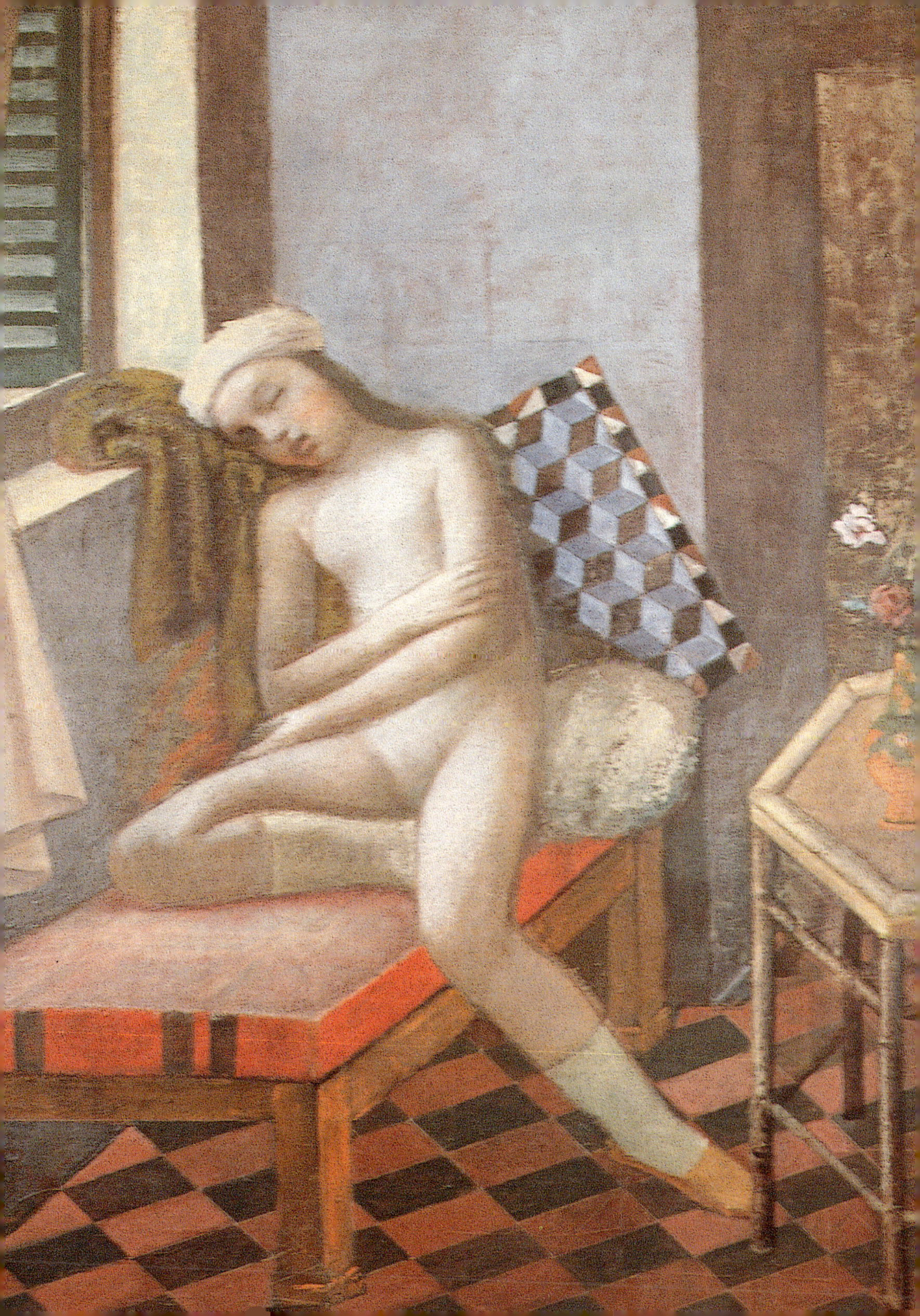

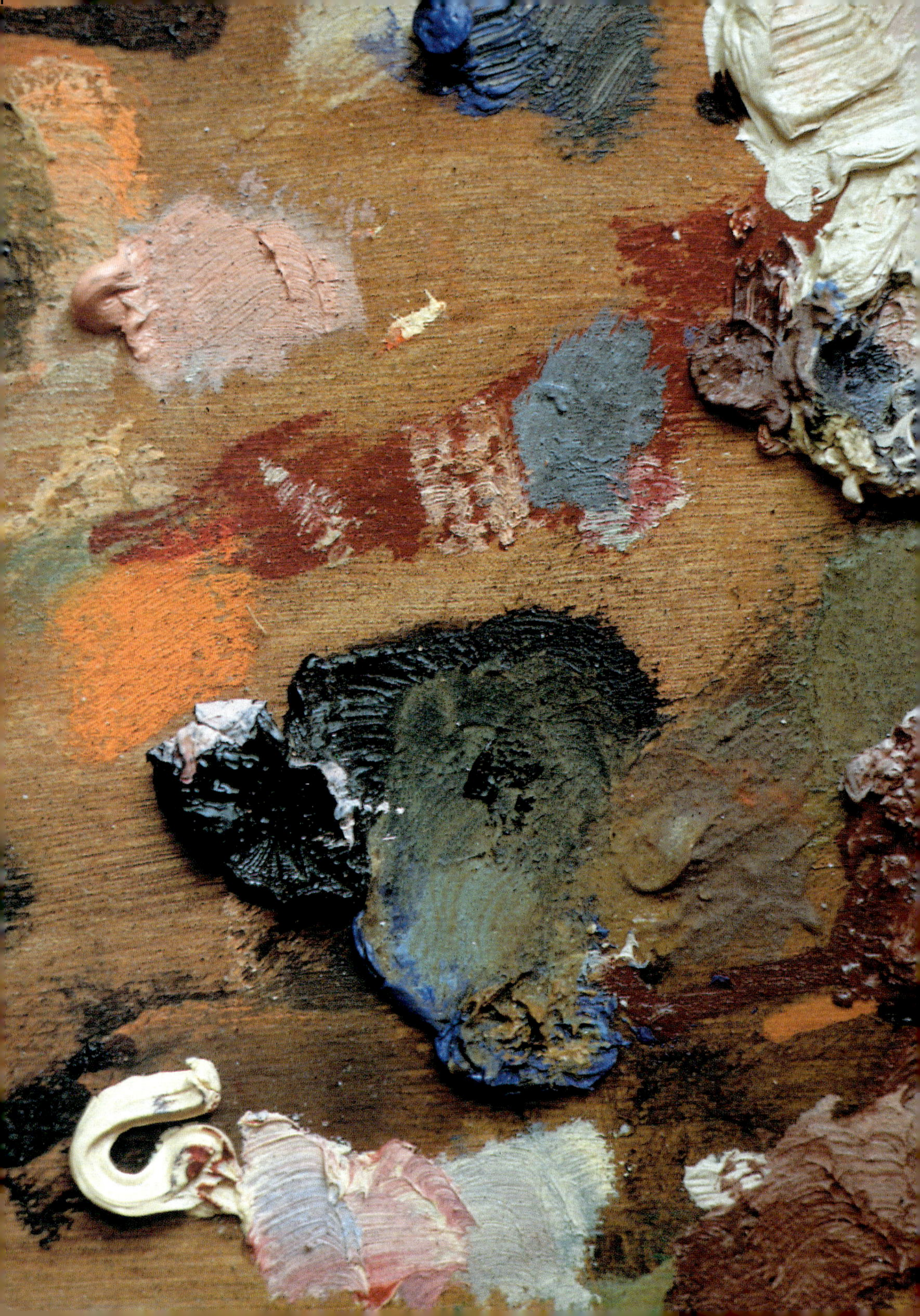

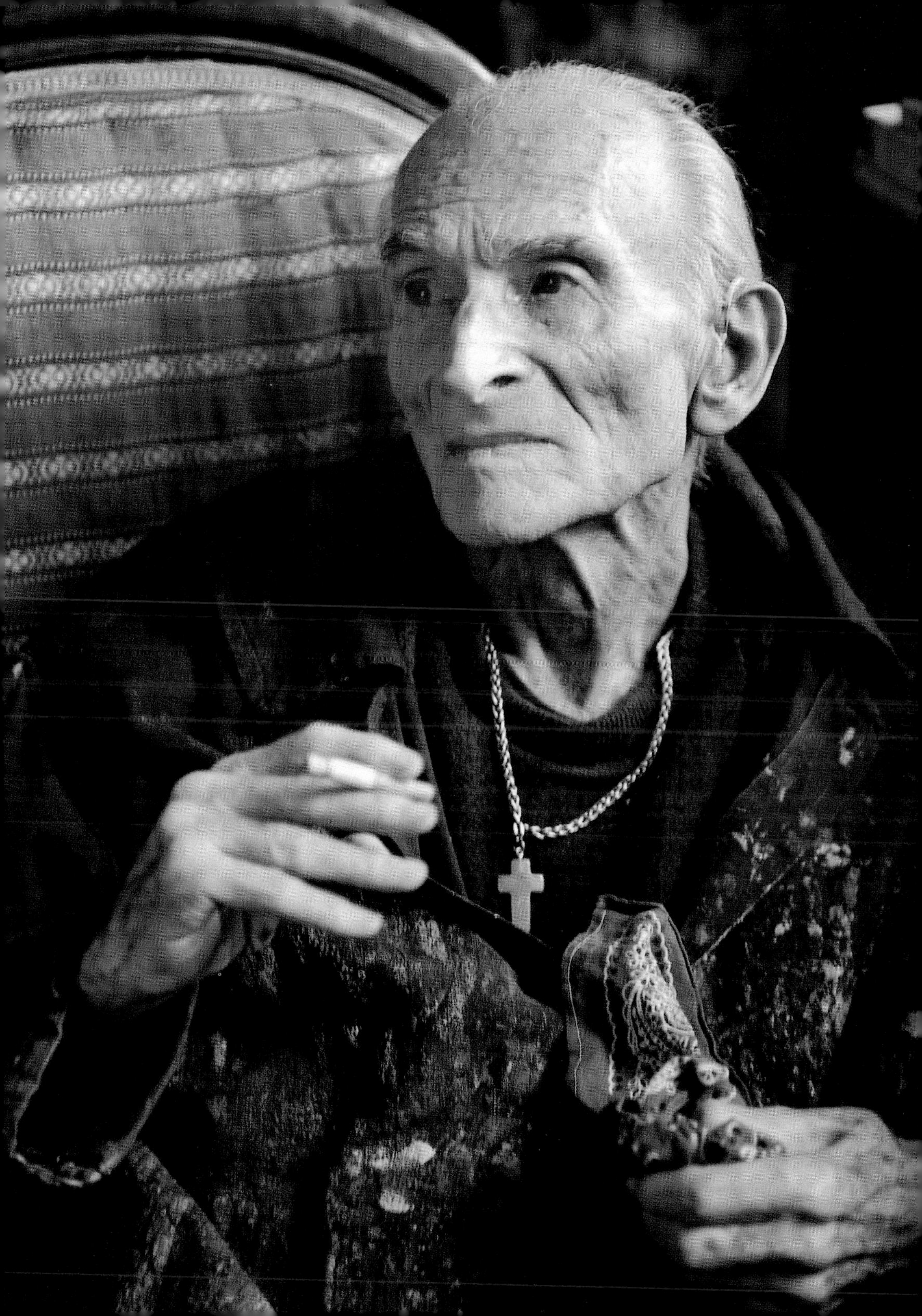

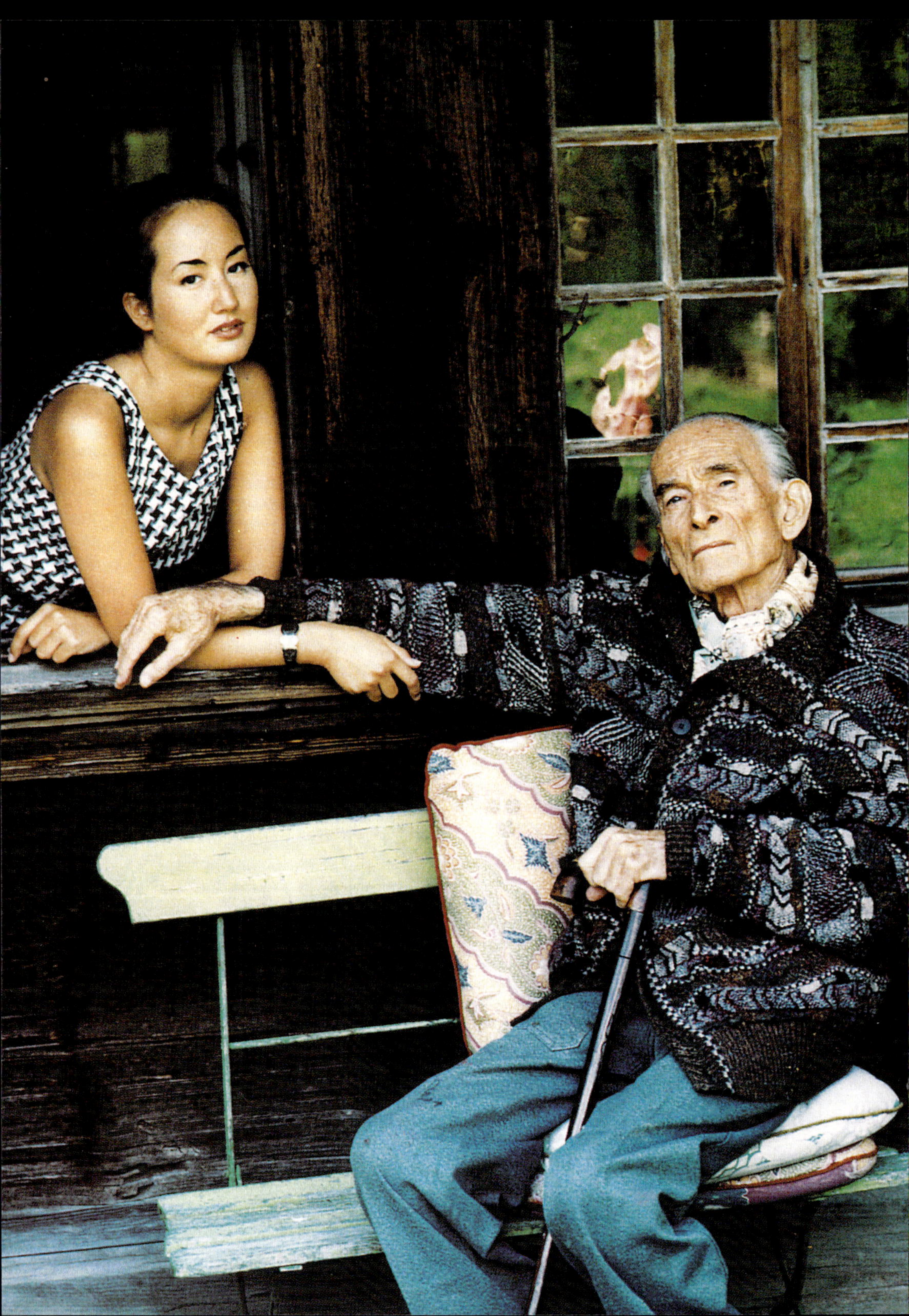

Chronology

1908: Balthus (Balthazar Klossowski de Rola) is born in Paris on February 29, the second son of Erich Klossowski (1875–1946), a Polish painter and art historian, and Baladine Klossowska (1886–1969), a painter.

1914: The family moves to Berlin.

1917: Baladine Klossowska de Rola moves to Geneva with her sons, Pierre and Balthazar.

1919: Attends the Lycée Calvin, Geneva, until 1921.
Baladine and Rainer Maria Rilke meet. Their friendship gives rise to substantial correspondence.

1921: Publication of an edition of Colette's novel *Mitsou* illustrated by Balthus: *Mitsou : Quarante images par Baltusz,* published by Rotapfed-Verlag (drawings in Indian ink with a preface by Rilke).
Baladine and her sons settle in Berlin.

1924: Joins his brother in Paris. On the advice of Bonnard, a friend of the family, he goes regularly to the Louvre to copy works by Poussin.

1925: Travels in Italy, to Florence and Arezzo, where he copies frescoes by Piero della Francesca, Masolino da Panicale and Masaccio, the Quattrocento painters.

1928–1929: Trips to Berlin and Zurich, Switzerland.

1930–1931: Military service in Morocco.

1932: Spends the summer in Bern, Switzerland, where he copies works by the Berliner painter Joseph Reinhart.
Returns to Paris in the fall, where he begins sketching the illustrations for Emily Bronte's novel *Wuthering Heights.*
Makes friends with André Derain and Pierre Jean Jouve.

1933: Moves to 4, rue de Furstenberg in Paris and paints *The Street.*
Makes friends with Antonin Artaud, Alberto Giacometti and Pierre Loeb, who later became his picture dealer.

1934: April 13–28, first one-man exhibition at the Galerie Pierre (Pierre Loeb).
Designs the sets and costumes for the play *As You Like It,* by Shakespeare.

1935: Designs the sets and costumes for the play *Les Cenci,* written and directed by Antonin Artaud.
Minotaure publishes reproductions of eight Balthus drawings for *Wuthering Heights.*

1936: Moves into a new studio in Cour de Rohan, in Paris, where he paints numerous portraits, including those of André Derain and Marie-Laure de Noailles.
Travels to London.

1937: Marries Antoinette de Watteville.

1938: First exhibition at the Pierre Matisse Gallery in New York—followed by six others until 1977.

With Harumi, his daughter, at Rossinière.

1939: Drafted, he returns to Paris.

1940–1941: Stays with his wife in Champrovent in Savoie, France.

1942: Stays in Bern and Friburg, Switzerland.

1945: Exhibition at Galerie Moos in Geneva. Moves into Villa Diodati in Geneva.

1946–1947: Exhibition at the Galerie des Beaux-Arts in Paris, organized by Henriette Gomès.

1948: Designs the sets and costumes for Albert Camus' play *L'Etat de Siège* and makes friends with André Malraux, Paul Eluard and Jean-Louis Barrault.

1950: Designs the sets and costumes for a production of Mozart's opera *Così fan Tutte* in Aix-en-Provence, France.

1953: Moves from Paris to the Château de Chassy in the Morvan, France.
Designs the sets and costumes for Ugo Betti's play *Delitto all'isola delle capre (Crime on Goat Island).*

1956: Exhibition at the Museum of Modern Art in New York.

1961–1976: Appointed director of the Villa Medici (the Académie de France in Rome).

1962: Trip to Japan, where he meets Setsuko Ideka.
Restoration of the Villa Medici.

1966: Exhibition at the Musée des Arts Décoratifs, Paris.

1967: Marries Setsuko.

1968: Exhibition at the Tate Gallery, London.

1969: Death of his mother.

1973: Restoration of the Villa Medici's gardens.

1977: Leaves Rome to settle in Switzerland, in the Grand Chalet at Rossinière.

1980: Twenty-six canvases are exhibited at the Venice Biennale, at the Scuola di San Giovanni Evangelista.

1983–1984: Retrospective in Paris, at the Musée national d'Art moderne, Centre Georges-Pompidou, which subsequently traveled to New York and Kyoto, Japan.

1993: Exhibition at the musée cantonal des Beaux-Arts in Lausanne, Switzerland, which later went to Tokyo.

1994: Retrospective at the Kunstmuseum in Bern, Switzerland.

1996: Retrospective at the Reina Sofia museum in Madrid, Spain.
Exhibition at the Villa Medici (Académie de France in Rome).

1999: Exhibition at the Musée des Beaux-Arts in Dijon, France.

2001: Dies on Sunday, February 18.

Girl in White, *1955, oil on canvas ($45^{1/2}$" x $34^{2/5}$").*
Private collection.

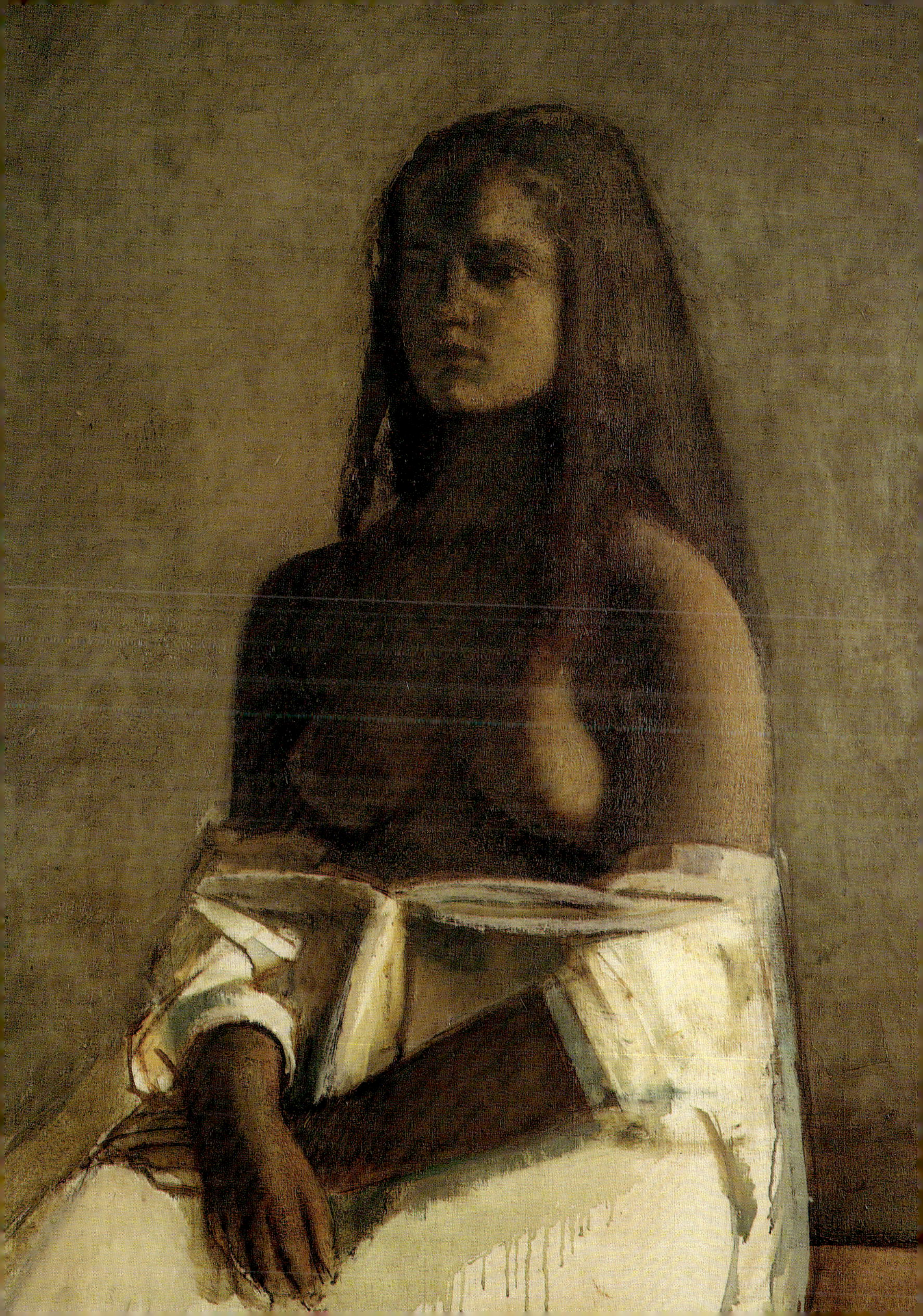

Balthus

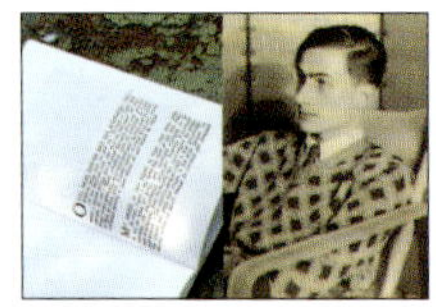

A page from Saint Augustin's *Confessions* (early 5th century), one of Balthus' bedside books. © L'Office/Photo: Dominique Issermann.
Balthus as a young man. © Archives Balthus. All rights reserved.

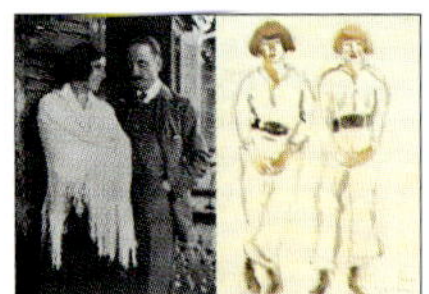

Baladine Klossowska, Balthus' mother, with Rainer Maria Rilke. © Centre Georges-Pompidou, Paris.
Balthus and his brother, watercolor by Baladine Klossowska. © Archives Balthus. All rights reserved.

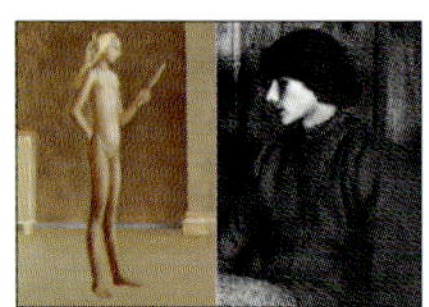

Nude with a Mirror, 1981–1983, oil on canvas (64″ x 51″). © Courtesy Galerie Alice Pauli, Lausanne.
Balthus as Romeo, age thirteen. © Archives Balthus. All rights reserved.

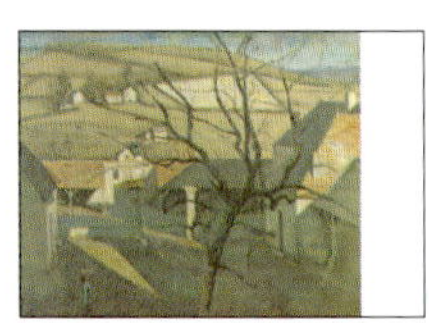

Farmyard at Chassy (Large Landscape with Tree), 1960, oil on canvas (51$^{1/3}$″ x 63$^{3/4}$″). Musée national d'Art moderne, Paris. © Centre Georges-Pompidou, Paris/Photo: Bertrand Prevost.

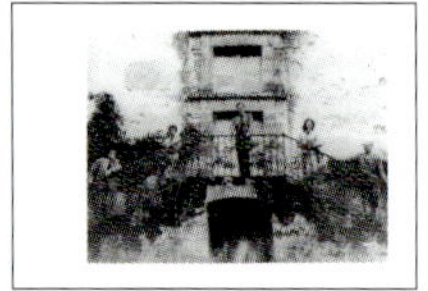

Alberto Giacometti, Mme. Matisse, Balthus, Annette Giacometti and Pierre Matisse *(from left to right),* circa 1955, in front of the Château de Chassy. © Centre Georges-Pompidou, Paris.

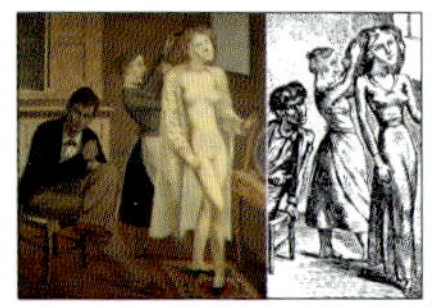

Cathy Dressing, 1933, oil on canvas (65″ x 62$^{1/2}$″). Musée national d'Art moderne, Paris. © Centre Georges-Pompidou, Paris.
Why have you that silk frock on, then…, illustration for Emily Bronte's *Wuthering Heights,* 1933, pen and ink (12$^{3/5}$″ x 11″). © Centre Georges-Pompidou, Paris.

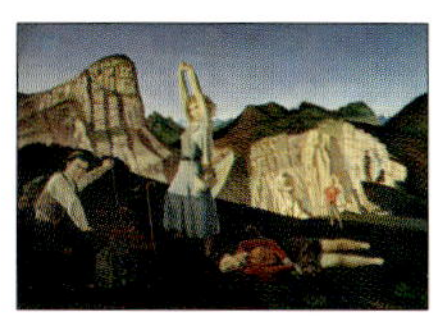

The Mountain, 1937, oil on canvas (98" x 144") The Metropolitan Museum of Art, New York. © 1986 The Metropolitan Museum of Art, New York.

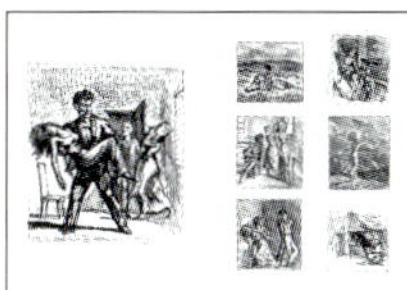

Illustrations for Emily Bronte's ***Wuthering Heights,*** 1933, pen and ink. Left: *Catherine's arms had fallen relaxed...* (11" x 9 4/5"). Right, from top to bottom: *But it was one of their chief amusements...* (10 3/5" x 12 2/5"); *Why have you that silk frock on, then...* (12 3/5" x 11"); *No, no, Isabella, you shan't run off...* (12" x 10 2/5"); *Cathy and I escaped...* (13 1/5" x 10 3/5"); *...and ran to seek for her friend herself...* (12 4/5" x 11"); *The room is haunted...* (8 1/2" x 9 9/10"). © Centre Georges-Pompidou, Paris.

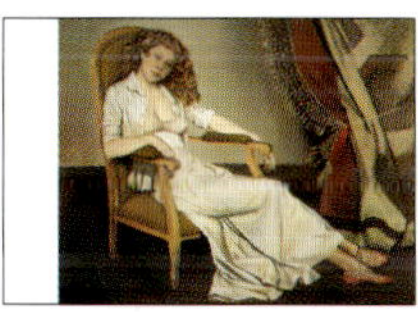

The White Skirt, 1937, oil on canvas (51 1/5" x 63 4/5"). Private collection. © Thomas Ammann Fine Art, Zurich.

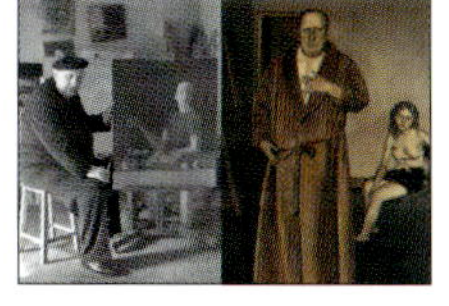

André Derain in his studio at Chambourcy, with the portrait of his niece, 1952. © Rue des Archives/Michel Sima Héritiers.
André Derain, 1936, oil on wood (44 2/5" x 28 1/2"). The Museum of Modern Art, New York. © 1999 The Museum of Modern Art, New York.

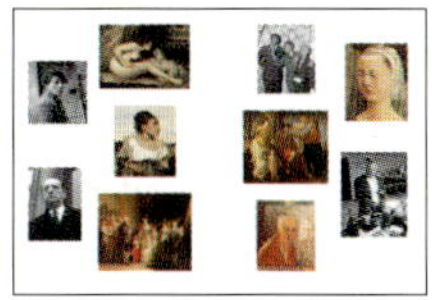

André Malraux; Alberto Giacometti; Pablo Picasso; Federico Fellini, Jean Cocteau and Giulietta Masina: © Rue des Archives; Goya, *Charles IV and His Family:* © AKG, Paris; Bonnard, *Self-portrait:* © AKG, Paris/2000 Adagp, Paris; Courbet, *Nude With a Dog:* © RMN/Photo: J. Schormans; Delacroix, *Orphan Girl at the Cemetery:* © RMN/Photo: Jean; Poussin, *The Inspiration of the Poet:* © RMN/PHOTO: R.G. Ojeda; Piero della Francesca, fresco, church of Arezzo (detail): © All rights reserved.

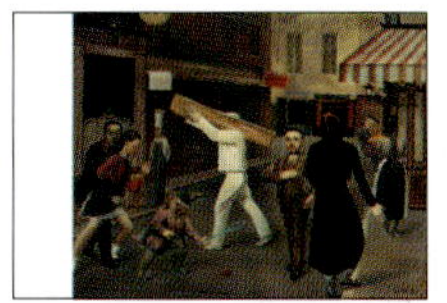

The Street, 1933, oil on canvas (76 3/4" x 94 1/2"). The Museum of Modern Art, New York. © 1999 The Museum of Modern Art, New York.

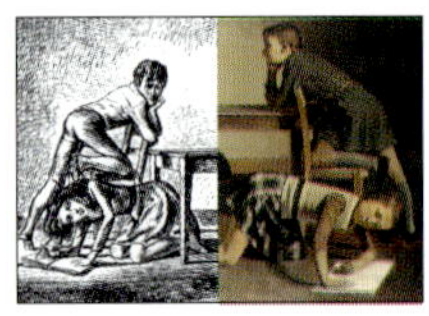

Because Cathy..., illustration for Emily Bronte's *Wuthering Heights*, 1933, pen and ink ($12^{2/5}$" x 10"). © Centre Georges-Pompidou, Paris.
The Children (Hubert and Marie-Thérèse Blanchard), 1937, oil on canvas ($49^{1/5}$" x $51^{1/5}$"). Musée Picasso, Paris. © RMN/Photo: J.G. Berizzi.

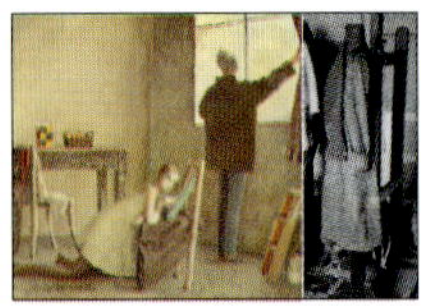

The Painter and His Model, 1980–1981, oil on canvas (89" x $90^{3/4}$"). Musée national d'Art moderne. © Centre Georges-Pompidou, Paris.
In the studio. © The Lefevre Gallery, Londres/Photo: Martin Summers.

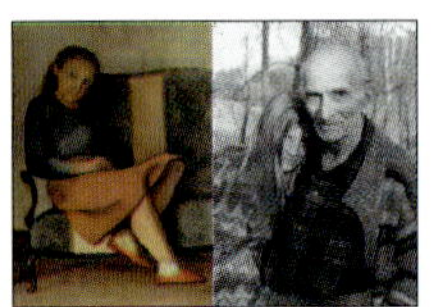

Colette sitting, 1954, oil on canvas ($31^{9/10}$" x $25^{3/5}$"). © Galerie Jan Krugier, Diteshiem & Cie, Geneva.
With Anna, daughter of the doctor at Rossinière and model for *Cat With Mirror III* and other paintings, 1994. © The Lefevre Gallery, London/Photo: Martin Summers.

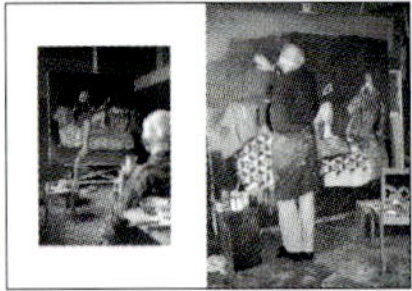

Balthus in his studio at Rossinière working on *Cat With Mirror III*, 1994.
© Photos: Giorgio Soavi.

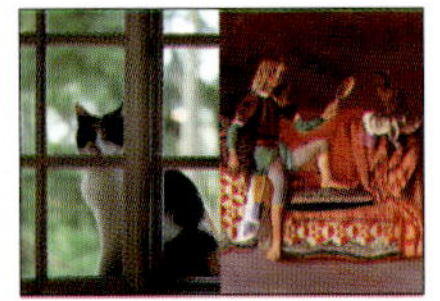

Mitsou, his cat. Throughout his life, Balthus always called one of his cats Mitsou. © L'Office/Photo: Dominique Issermann.
Cat With Mirror III, 1989–94, oil on canvas ($78^{3/4}$" x $76^{3/4}$"). © Courtesy Thomas Ammann Fine Art AG, Zurich, and The Lefevre Gallery, London.

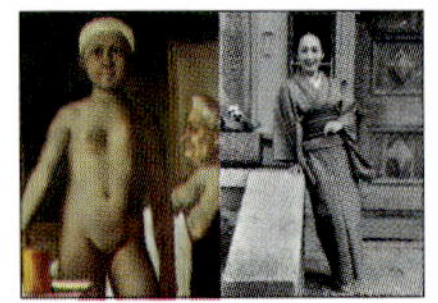

Young Girl Dressing, 1948, oil on canvas ($21^{4/5}$" x $18^{3/10}$"). Private collection. © Courtesy Galerie Jan Krugier, Ditesheim & Cie, Geneva.
Setsuko at Rossinière, 1994. © The Lefevre Gallery, London/Photo: Martin Summers.

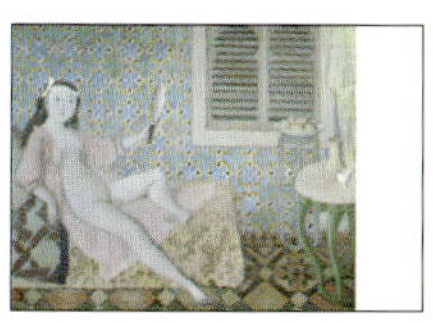

The Turkish Room, 1963–1966, casein and tempera on canvas ($70^{9/10}$" x $82^{3/5}$"). Musée national d'Art moderne, Paris. © Centre Georges-Pompidou, Paris.

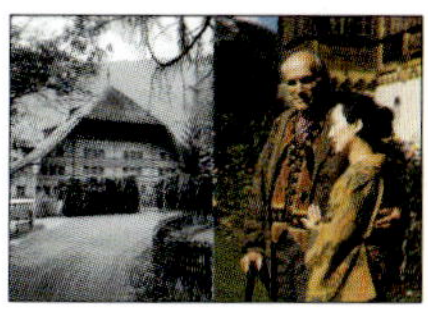

The Grand Chalet, Rossinière, 1994. © The Lefevre Gallery, London/Photo: Martin Summers.
With Setsuko at Rossinière. © Archives Balthus/All rights reserved.

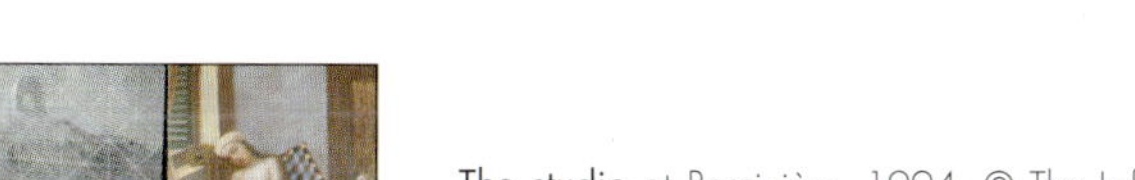

The studio at Rossinière, 1994. © The Lefevre Gallery, Londres/Photo: Martin Summers.
Nu assoupi, 1980, oil on canvas ($78^{3/4}$" x 59"). Private collection. © Centre Georges-Pompidou, Paris.

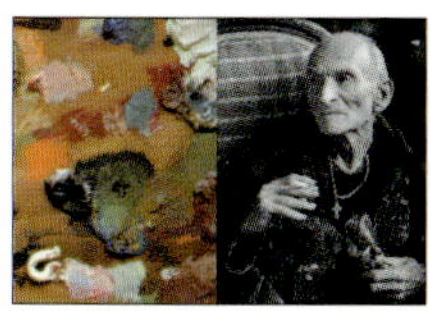

Balthus' palette. © L'Office/Photo: Dominique Issermann.
Balthus in Gstaad, 1997. © Photo: Bruce Weber.

The author and publisher would like to thank Count and Countess Klossowski de Rola and their daughter Harumi for their help preparing this book.
Our thanks to the photographers J.G. Berizzi, Dominique Issermann, Jean, R.G. Ojeda, Bertrand Prevost, J. Schormans, Giorgio Soavi, Martin Summers and Bruce Weber.
Our thanks also to Galerie Alice Pauli, Lausanne; Thomas Ammann Fine Art AG, Zurich; Jan Krugier, Ditesheim & Cie, Geneva; The Lefevre Gallery, London; the musée national d'Art moderne, Centre Georges-Pompidou, Paris; The Metropolitan Museum of Art, New York; The Museum of Modern Art, New York; to the photographic agencies AKG, Paris; L'Office, Paris; Rue des Archives Paris; and to the Photothèque de la RMN, Paris; and the Adagp, Paris.